THE ABOLITION OF PRISON

Jacques Lesage de La Haye
translated by Scott Branson

AK PRESS

The Abolition of Prison, Jacques Lesage de La Haye
© 2021 Jacques Lesage de La Haye
Translation © 2021 Scott Branson
This edition © 2021 AK Press (Chico / Edinburgh)
Originally published as *L'Abolition de la Prison* by Éditions Libertalia

ISBN: 9781849354202
E-ISBN: 9781849354219
Library of Congress Control Number: 2020946156

AK Press
370 Ryan Avenue #100
Chico, CA 95973
www.akpress.org
akpress@akpress.org

AK Press
33 Tower St.
Edinburgh EH6 7BN
Scotland
www.akuk.com
akuk@akpress.org

Please contact us to request the latest AK Press distribution catalog, which features
books, pamphlets, zines, and stylish apparel published and/or distributed by AK
Press. Alternatively, visit our websites for the complete catalog, latest news, and secure
ordering.

Cover design by Margaret Killjoy, birdsbeforethestorm.net
Printed in the United States of America on acid-free, recycled paper

For Angela Davis, Serge Livrozet, and Gabi Mouesca

Contents

Acknowledgments

My warmest thanks to Bernadette Porcher, Reichian analyst, for her translation from Spanish to French of Yoloth Fuentes Sanchez's memoir.

All of my political gratitude to Monique and Serge, hosts of the show, "Trous noirs" ["Black Holes"] on Radio libertaire (89.4), for the extensive material they supplied me with on the community police and community security, justice, and reeducation system in the State of Guerrero in Mexico—the society against the State.

Finally, I have a special gratitude for Floréal, whose corrections, professional as well as political, were invaluable.

Introduction

Why bother with prisons? Typically, it's only those on the prison staff who talk about it. Occasionally, a philosopher or sociologist will take interest. Or maybe you are an anti-prison militant. As for prisoners, most of them quickly flee the grounds, wanting to move on once and for all.

In my case, I wanted to remain part of struggle to improve the conditions of incarceration and to work towards the abolition of prison. Having served a long prison sentence, I understand how harmful this institution is.

Though I was born into an aristocratic family, I still collected all of the traits that end up making hooligans and thieves: an absent father—a master mariner, who traveled across all the oceans and was physically present only two months a year. An overwhelmed mother, who saw herself as a martyr and violently beat her two eldest sons.

My brother Jean-Paul and I formed a gang of very young delinquents. I was seventeen and he was sixteen. We began by stealing cars and motorcycles, then we shifted to higher gears: break-ins and hold-ups, with two other young people our age.

When we were arrested in 1957, the psychiatrists diagnosed my brother as schizophrenic and me as psychopathic. In my case, they weren't wrong. The psychopath lives in such despair that there is no other option than acting out. For Jean-Paul, they made a mistake. The schizophrenic is totally cut off from reality, whereas the paraphrenic has a narrow margin of adjustment with delusions, which was my brother's case. But he clearly fell within the diagnosis of psychosis.

In any case, Jean-Paul did not recover from incarceration, since at the end of eighteen months of confinement, he told me that he was the Antichrist and was going to announce the apocalypse. That got him twenty years behind bars, if you add up the joint and the asylum. He was destroyed by electroshocks, insulin comas, and heavy chemotherapy. And thus he died at fifty-one, fourteen years after his final release.

We had a difficult argument on which we never agreed. To survive, Jean-Paul prescribed to weightlifting and masturbation. I agreed with him, except that I also believed it was necessary to study. It seemed essential to me to have diplomas in order to find work when we were released, especially if we were over thirty—which seemed pretty old to me!

I stuck to my program, though it cost me enormously, since the prison administration put significant obstacles in my way. It took three years for me to get permission to get my high school diploma. I had worked tirelessly for it. As for my university studies, it was even worse because I could not carry out the practical laboratory work.

After first choosing philosophy, I eventually switched to psychology when I saw my brother deteriorate. Additionally, I saw many people who were incarcerated commit suicide or become mentally ill. One person thought he heard his wife making love with a sergeant named Trotinette on the loudspeaker in his cell.

When I received my B.A. in psychology under the old university system, I decided to pursue a doctoral degree. I chose the subject, "The psychological effects of emotional and sexual deprivation on the incarcerated individual." To gather the material needed for this work, I had to interview comrades, so I requested permission from the central prison management in Caen. The authorities didn't design to answer but sent the chief supervisor who was given with the duty of telling me, "Lesage, there is no way that you will write a thesis on this subject. That could be done by a psychiatrist, a teacher—or if need be, by me." I appreciated his extreme modesty!

Therefore, I had to carry out my research in secret. I was unaware how much risk I took. Fortunately, a new director arrived, Pierre Campinchi, who was quite surprised to hear I was threatened with disciplinary transfer in thirty-five reports by overseers that stated I took notes on the benches of the walking area and sports grounds. When I explained the situation to him, he moved me from cellblock B to cellblock C, which was called "Improvement."

He requested an authorization for my doctoral thesis from the minister and obtained it. Then he removed me from the furniture workshop with the bad incarcerated people, and appointed me as librarian. Finally, after I'd served eleven and a half of my twenty years, and with two attempts, Campinchi was able get me parole!

Pierre Campinchi's existence helped me avoid the worst, which would have led me to spend even more years behind bars. But one individual doesn't make up the system. I left prison convinced that I needed to fight against this unjust institution. Very soon, I joined the Prison Information Group [Groupe information prison—GIP], with Michel Foucault, and the intellectuals, then the Prisoner Action Committee [Comité d'action des prisonniers—CAP], with Serge Livrozet.

I still needed to finish my studies in psychology, which I had never completed due to university reforms and challenges from the prison. To make a living while waiting for my graduate diploma, I had to work as a laborer, docker, market hauler, a mover with Manpower, and a bouncer at Golf Drouot, the well-known discotheque owned by Henri Leproux.

I became a psychologist at the psychiatric hospital in Ville-Évrard and taught courses in psychology at University Paris-VIII—Vincennes from 1972–2003. Since 1989, I have also hosted the radio show "Ras les murs" [Tear down the walls] on Radio libertaire (89.4), in order to continue the anti-prison struggle with resolve. It is in this spirit that I published more than twenty books, including *La Machine à fabriquer les délinquants* [*The*

3

Delinquent-Making Machine], *La Guillotine du sexe* [*The Punishment of Sex*]—which is an adaptation of my doctoral thesis that the prison didn't allow me to defend—*L'Homme de metal* [*Metal Man*], and *La Mort de l'asile* [*The Death of the Asylum*].

With *The Abolition of Prison*, I complete this line of thought: Prison ought to be deconstructed in order to never be reconstructed.

CHAPTER ONE

Why Prisons?

A society that locks people up reveals its fear and its incompetence—and therefore, its failure.

The same is true if it employs exile. Even worse if exile is compounded with imprisonment, like in Guyana and New Caledonia at the time of the penal colony. In the ancient customs of African tribes, this practice was inhumane without being barbaric. The exiled person had nearly no chance of escaping. But they weren't killed, mutilated, or broken.

In this regard, Western countries have proven to be among the worst, using torture and execution. That is why Michel Foucault could speak of the "gentle way in punishment" when prison replaced torture and execution. He refers to the stance of the Chancellery in 1789: "Let penalties be regulated and proportional to the offenses, let the death sentence be passed only on those convicted of murder, and let the tortures that revolt humanity be abolished."[1] We still have a long way to go, since we have yet to abolish the death penalty. Although it disappeared from France's repressive arsenal in 1981, it continues to be used all around the world. Under the most basic ethics, it should be unimaginable that a country execute an individual on the basis that this person murdered someone. A civilization that claims a high level of humanity must not enforce the law of retaliation. Or else, where is the example, the lesson, offered to the population?

"The Ten Commandments" say, "Thou shall not kill." Thus, those who enforce this law should not break it. In fact, the death penalty is forbidden on principle, except when it comes the rulers. This means that it is really the law of the strongest. Under no circumstances is it justice.

In 1764, Cesare Beccaria wrote: "It appears absurd to me that the laws, which are the expression of the public will and which detest and punish homicide, commit murder themselves, and, in order to dissuade citizens from assassination, command public assassination."[2] And yet we still have to investigate the vexing question of the origin of prison. We can't help but note that as soon as people began constructing buildings with doors that closed, they began to confine the people that disturbed them. But this was not systematic, nor even state sponsored. However, history shows us that under the monarchy, people with "loose" morals or who had incurred debts could be snatched away to places like the Bastille. And for a long time during the Middle Ages there were dungeons in many of the fortresses . . .

A brutal way of dealing with criminals was to send them to the galleys. This penalty was established in 1560 by Charles X. The strength of these miserable people was used to propel warships. They were handled with the worst violence. They were beaten violently by the overseers. But sails turned out to be more efficient than oars, which is why Louis XV allowed the end to the galleys in 1748. They were replaced by forced labor at the ports in Brest, Rochefort, and Toulon.

During the Revolution, the Constitutional Assembly placed the handling of criminals and mentally ill people in separate institutions. Dominique Vernier explains: "In France, prison as place to serve time was established by the criminal code in October 1791."[3]

But, aside from the fact that it was supposed to protect society from a person likely to commit offenses and crimes, what was its true mission? To deliver justice? Clearly not, since the era was steeped in religion, the spirit of vengeance, sadism, and voyeurism. The one certainty is that for a while, the delinquent is prevented from harming. Their isolation provides a feeling of minimal security for the witnesses of the offence.

So can it truly be about the force of example? Certainly not, for prison has never deterred anyone. If it was effective, crime would have become scarce bit by bit, until it disappeared. This has never happened anywhere— just as the death sentence has never stopped crimes, and above all, murders. If anything, when the execution was public, an atmosphere of sadistic and perverse enjoyment prevailed in the crowd. We can't forget the excited spectators who dipped their handkerchiefs in the blood of the victim in the place de Grève.

Well, does prison at least allow the criminal to be educated? Does it strive towards their "reformation," their reintegration or re-entry? None of these, despite the attempts made for their supposed improvement. We are constantly reminded by the suicide rate (seven times higher in prison than in society) and the recidivism rate (50 percent and higher depending on the categories of crime). As Dominique Vernier writes: "Recidivism is a measure of the ineffectiveness of prison for two reasons. First, it indicates that the stay in prison did not help stem the desire to commit offenses, nor did it provide a new situation in which the individual is no longer tempted to commit them. Second, this stay did not act as a deterrent."[4]

Building on this line of thinking, Peter Kropotkin goes even further: "You can hang, draw and quarter the murderers as much as you like, but the number of murders will not diminish. On the other hand, if you abolish the death penalty there will not be a single murder more. Statisticians and legists know that when the severity of the penal code is lessened there is never an increase in the number of attempts against the lives of citizens."[5]

Phillippe Paraire translated Kropotkin's book *In Russian and French Prisons* (published in London in 1887) from English. Commenting on Kropotkin's ideas in the introduction, Paraire remarks: "According to him, the social exclusion of criminals through imprisonment and of the mentally ill through institutionalization should be replaced by freedom, while building support networks, and also professional and educational reintegration. . . This is truly a visionary idea of the law's efforts at correction."[6]

But the considerations of the anarchist thinker go much further. Though he was, of course, treated like a utopian in the nineteenth century, Kropotkin is a forerunner, believing that only a true social revolution can bring the end of punishment by imprisonment. He argues this with evidence that we clearly recognize today, but that few politicians, even on the left, truly dare to support: "Two-thirds of all breaches of law being so called 'crimes against property,' these cases will disappear, or be limited to a quite trifling amount, when property, which is now the privilege of the few, shall return to its real source, the community."[7] We have unfortunately not yet reached this stage of our evolution. Claiming to condemn a theory that promotes violence, chaos, and disorder, property owners refuse to recognize the truth. They cling firmly to their privileges: money, power, and property.

The great antiracist, feminist, and anti-prison militant Angela Davis gets straight to the point: "The prison therefore functions ideologically as an abstract site into which undesirables are deposited, relieving us of the responsibility of thinking about the real issues afflicting those communities from which prisoners are drawn in such disproportionate numbers."[8] She points specifically to racism and globalized capitalism. This inevitably leads us to look at economic poverty and cultural exclusion.

Interviewed by Davis, Assata Shakur mentions a shameful practice, officially forbidden today in France but that continues nonetheless to hold sway here and there: "The 'internal search' was as humiliating and disgusting as it sounded. You sit on the edge of this table and the nurse holds your legs open and sticks a finger in your vagina and moves it around. She has a plastic glove on. Some of them try to put one finger in your vagina and another one up your rectum at the same time."[9]

We will avoid endlessly reproducing examples. This does not even require commentary. However, it is truly alarming that the violence, the brutality, the ineffectiveness, not to mention the uselessness and harmfulness of prison, have been demonstrated since the beginning of the nineteenth century. Michel Foucault recalls: "For the prison, in its reality and visible effects, was condemned immediately as the great failure of penal justice."[10] He adds: "the critique of the prison and its methods appeared very early on, in those same years 1820–45; indeed, it was embodied in a number of formulations which—figures apart—are today repeated almost unchanged."[11]

Dostoevsky makes this shining statement of truth: "I am firmly convinced that the results achieved even by the much-vaunted cell-system are superficial, deceptive, and illusory. It sucks the living sap out of a person, wears down their spirit, weakens and browbeats them, and then presents the shriveled, half-demented mummy as a pattern of repentance and reform."[12] Obviously, he isn't even speaking about people who go back inside.

We can only agree with Victor Hugo's view: "Moreover, we seek not merely the abolition of the death penalty, we want a complete reworking of punishment in all its forms, from the highest to the lowest, from the lock to the chopper; and time is an element which should enter into such an undertaking, in order that it may be well done."[13]

Evolution is slow. But prison is so outdated and brutal that it will take even longer to make it disappear if we don't manage to destroy it through an anarchist social revolution. The final return of prisoners from Guyana only happened in 1953. And the regime of partial release only truly began to be implemented, case by case, in 1958.[14]

Despite a variety of improvements, we must unfortunately remember that the disastrous maximum security and closed security wings were established in 1975, right after the uprisings of 1974. But it should be noted that solitary confinement—in all its forms—has always existed behind bars.

It is a serious concern that, one after another, efforts at removal, adding up to a slow death, have been created, like in 1994, the thirty-year prison sentence and life without parole. Under such circumstances, where repressive measures are added to each other, the family life units established in 2003, seem merely like a window dressing or sham.

The law of preventative detention, in 2008, goes beyond the limit. Following a primarily psychiatric medical examination, prisoners are labeled dangerous and susceptible of recidivism. They are kept in prison in order to prevent any future possibility of crime. They then have to wait a year before a multidisciplinary commission decides whether they must remain in detention.

The loss of all hope is an oft-recurring theme in the protests of people who are incarcerated. In 1977, Taleb Hadjadj wrote: "The outcome is either an act of desperation, or mental illness like paranoia or schizophrenia."[15] For him, this is suicide. Serge Coutel, another person serving a life sentence, tells us: "This tired justice is the most terrible institution of our time, far worse than the crime it claims to punish. Yes, it no longer crucifies, no longer burns at the stake, and no longer decapitates. There is no longer iron, wheel, gallows, pyre, nothing. Time replaces everything. A life dismembered by time! That's prison: time nakedly meted out. They don't kill. They let die."[16]

The prisoners of Clairvaux issued the Call of the Ten in 2006: "We, the living beings locked up for life in the highest security penitentiary center in France (yet none of us as horrible as a Papon),[17] we call for the effective reinstatement of the death penalty for us."[18]

In answer to the clumsy and stupid response by Pascal Clément, the minister of justice, one of the signers, Abdelhamid Hakkar, desperately drives the point home: "I dare you to come back here with the guillotine, I'll give myself up. But I do not resign myself to a fate of being buried alive."[19]

Well known for his spectacular escapes—especially from the Santé prison in a helicopter piloted by his wife Liliane—Michael Vaujour insightfully analyzes the deadly effects of incarceration: "And then you see, you feel, you realize again your slow decay, as much psychic as intellectual or physical, and through its excessiveness it makes you mad with icy rage."[20]

A definitive text by Nathalie Ménignon, recalling Ulrike Meinhof, follows Michel Vaujour's description to its logical conclusion: "You 'see' day and night without truly distinguishing one from the other. You lose time, you lose desire, and finally you lose yourself. That is what solitary confinement is like, the annihilation of your human, social behavior, and of your internal being, aiming at the splitting of body and soul by the death of your reflexive unity, of your identity."[21]

What options are there when the disaster is of such proportions? We know it well: madness, suicide, or escape. These are the constants that endlessly return, once we begin to discuss prison even a little bit.

Michel Foucault, a philosopher well-known for his militant commitments, was not afraid to make this conclusion, similarly to Jean-Paul Sartre: "Nobody should make themselves the accomplice of those that deliberately expose them to a harmful future. Escape in this case is a duty."[22]

The great revolutionary militant Victor Serge can beautifully close out this series of analyses on imprisonment with a paradox: "Modern prisons are imperfectible, since they are perfect. There is nothing left but to destroy them."[23] As an anarchist, then communist, and finally anti-Stalinist, Serge knows what he is talking about. Just like Kropotkin, he knew the Russian and French jails. The communists could not bear that he became a Trotskyist and the Trotskyists could not bear that he was communist. In France, he was unjustly accused of being a member of the anarchist bank robbers. What's more, he refused to snitch on his friends ... He has a conclusive view of jails, prisons, and penal colonies: "Prison is made to kill."[24]

CHAPTER TWO

The Revolt of the Abolitionists

Over the centuries, people's attitudes about prison have changed and they are perceived as more and more inhumane. This realization has occurred gradually. First we had to get rid of the death penalty, the most obvious legacy of cruelty. If we follow the movement of history, it is clear that prison is the alternative to execution. But is it any wonder that its logical conclusion is to become a slow death penalty?

In 1981, France abolished the death penalty, a strong message sent to the world. But let's not gloat; other countries came before us. The idea made headway, but with reluctance. However, the movement for the abolition of capital punishment is very powerful. It is a struggle pursued with determination, and the strongholds have surrendered one after the other: If life is the supreme value, what right do we have to put an end to it? It has been continually proven that the death penalty doesn't work as an example—hardly anyone is deterred by it. Alas, there is still intense resistance to its abolition in a number of countries including China, Japan, Iran, Iraq, Saudi Arabia, the United States, Turkey, Nigeria, and so many others.

The more the death penalty vanishes, the more visible prison becomes. The argument for it is wildly inconsistent. Prison is supposedly the only way of dissuading delinquents and criminals: when the "bad guys" are behind bars, good people can sleep at night. Prison is supposedly the ultimate guarantee of security. As Farid Ben Rhadi, former prisoner and host of the radio show "Ras les murs" on Radio libertaire (89.4), puts it: "Prison only exists to make those on the outside believe they are free."

There are other voices—not only of those who have been incarcerated—who condemn the outdated, destructive monster of prison. The reformist position is the most widespread. That doesn't prevent a more and more multifaceted tendency from making its voice heard. The Quaker movement was founded in Great Britain by George Fox in 1647, and today has a significant presence in the United States. An austere protestant movement, Quakerism upholds pacifism and solidarity. Quakers helped many people who were forced into slavery flee the plantations in the southern United States and settle in Canada. Quakerism's aspirations for freedom makes it one of the predecessors of the prison abolition movement.

In the beginning of the twentieth century, the Anarchist Red Cross called forcefully and decisively for the abolition of prisons. An association of political support for anarchist prisoners, it changed its name after the Russian revolution of 1917, and has since been called the Anarchist Black Cross. It didn't want to be confused with the International Red Cross, and especially want to avoid *red*, the symbol of violence and dictatorship. After Bakunin, the anarchists continued to part ways with Marx and the communists.

In March 1984, the sociologist Catherine Baker published an abolitionist manifesto, in which she articulated an explicitly radical idea: "The principles that established prison were philanthropic principles. Criminals, during incarceration, were supposed to reflect and mend their ways. History proved this to be tedious nonsense. We are supposed to build on absolute intellectual rigor, and yet prison is based on the hope that things will be better after—that is, it is based on total nonsense."[1] At the Amsterdam Abolitionist Conference in June 1985, Catherine Baker delivered a talk called, *Does Prison Abolition Mean the Abolition of Justice, Rights, and All Society?* In it, she offered essential insights, such as this particular reflection: "prison is an ideal death since it eliminates as a whole those whom society would only be able to physically kill in very small numbers. It's an emotional cost-cutting."[2] Catherine Baker's work is at the same time ethical, philosophical, and political: "We want to destroy prison, both because the society we are in is a prison and because the prison we are in is not a society."[3] She echoes science fiction authors who describe societies that don't have prisons because they have become giant prisons.

At the same moment in 1985, the Magistrate Trade Union approved a motion for prison abolition at its annual conference.[4] Of course, that didn't pass without controversy, which caused much ink to flow.

In February 2001, the team from *L'Envolée*[5] (a journal and a radio show on Fréquence Paris Plurielle 106.3), started a movement called "To End All Prisons." It brought together "Ras les murs"; the Movement of Immigration and Banlieues (MIB [Mouvement de l'immigration et des banlieues]); Act Up's prison committee; Ban Public [public announcement, information on prisons in Europe]; the prison committee of the union CNT [National Confederation of Labor, anarcho-syndicalist union]; the collective Ne Laissons Pas Faire [We Won't Let It Happen]; the Basque and Corsican prisoner support collective; and even more groups. The meetings continued through November. Political differences made it impossible for the various participants to reach agreement, but in 2009 *L'Envolée* published, *Peines éliminatoires et isolement carceral, Pour en finir avec toutes les prisons [Perpetual Sentences and Solitary Confinement: To End All Prisons]*, which serves as wonderful culmination of this stormy experiment.[6]

In 2014, Samuel Gautier, an ex-prison nurse and member of the Observatoire international des prisons [International Prison Watchdog group (OIP)], published an article on the Mediapart site, titled "Abolir les prisons, ses mécanismes et ses logiques" ["Abolish Prison, Its Processes, and Its Logic"]. He quoted Catherine Baker's manifesto, hoping to add his own perspective to hers. He added important details that leave no room for ambiguity. He highlights: "In the case of misdemeanor: solitary is effectively a hole where the incarcerated person is reduced to the status of an animal." He adds: "Solitary confinement is white torture that breaks down bit by bit." The conclusion is straightforward: "Prison is a prime example of something you cannot try to reform, but must instead eliminate."[7]

He is not far from Victor Serge's opinion. All of the commentators and researchers share a single argument: "It must be permanently removed because all studies have shown that imprisonment inevitably fails to prevent recidivism and costs society far more than it contributes to it."[8]

Professionals of the prison system—as well as prisoners of it—say: "Those subjected to what we today call 'long sentences' are people who are simply condemned to a slow death penalty, a social death penalty." Samuel Gautier's statement reminds us that more than three thousand people have committed suicide since 1977, the date the last person was sentenced to death in France . . . This should raise an ethical problem for us.

"We claim that it won't be long before prison will be seen by people as the irrefutable symptom of the state of brutality, the backwardness of moral standards and feelings, in which humanity lived in the 20th century and even at the beginning of the 21st century."[9] A number of us former prisoners signed this statement, including Audrey Chenu, author of *Girlfight*; Philippe El Sehnnawy; the unknown con, author of the blog of the same name on Rue 89 Lyon; Gabriel Mouesca, former president of OIP. But also Philippe Bouvet, professor of history and geography, and moreover, father of an incarcerated person; Alain Cangina, president of the association Rebirth PJ2R [for a resilient and reconciling justice]; Lucie Davy, lawyer; Tony Ferri, philosopher; Samuel Gautier, with his new role as a documentary filmmaker; Yanis Lantheaume, lawyer; Thierry Lodé, biologist; Noël Mamère, politician; Yann Moulier-Boutang, economist and essayist; Michel Onfray, philosopher; and Antoine Paris, journalist.

To round out these ideas, it would be helpful to refer to the authors most likely to argue directly against imprisonment. Some of them have fought as militants, but there are others who were seized by the subject without coming up through the ranks of the anti-prison combat.

One of the oldest to have addressed the issue is Peter Kropotkin. As an anarchist thinker, he couldn't accept the idea that the State deprives a human being of liberty under the pretext of punishment or even of education. The key to his philosophy is stated at the end of the book *In Russian and French Prisons* (published first in London in 1887): "Liberty and collective care have proved the best cure."[10]

Kropotkin concludes thus: "All that tends this way will bring us nearer to the solution of the great question which has not ceased to preoccupy human societies since the remotest antiquity, and which cannot be solved by prisons."[11]

In 1975, the American psychologist Dennie Briggs published *In Place of Prison*. In it, he speaks of a "project of new career development," which he created in 1965 with the sociologist Douglas Grant in the state of Massachusetts. Instead of going to prison, youth were placed in foster homes and families. The recidivism rate, which had reached 45 percent among those who were incarcerated, fell to 10.5 percent for the others. The alternative proved its worth. Dennie Briggs concludes: "three states have set about deliberately closing all or most of their prisons for youth. California has halved its number of youths in confinement; Florida is close behind. Massachusetts has had no youth prisons in operation since 1972."[12]

He leaves us with a surreal image: "200 men still on duty in the empty prisons of Massachusetts."[13] That was true in 1980, but what about today?

In *Peines perdues* [*Lost Causes* (1982)], Louk Hulsman, with the help of Jacqueline Bernat de Celis, offers an argument inspired by the Bantu thinking that replaces punishment with mediation and reparation.[14] He explains: "The consequences of a murder are civil, not penal, and harmony comes not from punishment but from reparation."[15] The authors recommend the abolition of the penal system, which would make the institution of prison obsolete . . .

Catherine Baker follows in Louk Hulsman's footsteps with *L'Abolition de la prison* [*The Abolition of Prison* (1985)] and *Pourqoui faudrait-il punir* [*Why Must We Punish?* (2004)]. The subtitle of the second book (*Sur l'abolition du système penal* [*On the abolition of the penal system*]) goes in the same direction. The goal is clearly stated: "The idea of outright abolition makes headway despite the grim era we are in—and often because of it."[16] Catherine Baker discusses a historical fact: "The Truth and Reconciliation Commission put in place by Desmond Tutu caused a true revolution in the standard judicial system. On the condition of publicly admitting their crime in a face-to-face interview with the family of the victim, the guilty person was assured of not being sentenced and allowed to leave free."[17]

She repeats the argument of militant democrats: "We cannot guarantee life while putting to death; we cannot defend liberty while imprisoning thousands of individuals; we cannot reject violence while using violence."[18]

The debate "Prison and Anarchy" was organized in Paris in 1991 by the "Ras les murs" team. It gave rise to a pamphlet, *Déviance en société libertaire* [*Deviance in an Anarchist Society*], published in 1993. There once again, reparation replaced imprisonment. A new idea emerged: "In a place that would not be a prison, of course, but a communal house, people from the town would be able to enter and to leave much more freely, including the deviants. Thus, a great deal of the work of pedagogical, psychological, intellectual and political exchange could be done in a flexible, broad, and diverse manner."[19] It's a prophetic idea, though it is already the current practice in a whole community of villages of Indigenous people in Guerrero, Mexico.

Albert Jacquard, the geneticist, has always worked towards more freedom. In 1993, he published *Un Monde sans prison* [*A World Without Prison*]. The ideas in this book attest to the depth of his thought: "The search for immediate security creates long term insecurity."[20] He joins Louk Hulsman, Catherine Baker, and the Indigenous people of Guerrero: "In a community, why not invite the concerned parties to get together in order to find a way of repairing a harm committed?"[21] He repeats what many others have demonstrated. Prison is expensive and creates recidivism. Thus, his final point: "A society without prison can only be a society that doesn't need prisons."[22] All the anarchists agree in saying that prison cannot disappear without a radical change of society taking place. Albert Jacquard notes: "The disappearance of prisons can only be the result of a deep transformation involving our ideas of guilt, punishment, discipline, and especially of the place that we give each person in the work of human collectivity."[23] Hence, his philosophy: "Let us not only imagine a society without prisons, but a society without violence, a society of justice, with respect for each individual."[24]

Today the anti-prison fight continues to evolve. It is fashionable for depressed militants to say that it has lost its momentum. They forget that we have twenty radio stations in France that broadcast shows about prison. It's true that there aren't really collectives like the Groupe information prison [Prison Information Group (GIP)] and the Comité d'action des prisonniers [Committee of Prisoner Action (CAP)] any more. Nonetheless, what we do still have in this area comes from the work of GIP and CAP. The OIP, obligated to neutrality by its status as an NGO, still regularly refers to this work: the militants of CAP, like Serge Livrozet, whose groundbreaking book, *De la prison à la révolte* [*From Prison to Revolt*], has been reprinted five times, conclusively demonstrated how to deconstruct prison towards its ultimate abolition.

In the second issue of the *Journal of Prisoners*, published by CAP in January 1973, eleven points were outlined. They became the standard platform of demands, taken up again and demanded by many prisoners in the following years:

1. Erasure of criminal record
2. Removal of denial of entry
3. End of death penalty
4. End of life in prison
5. End to criminal guardianship (relegation)
6. End to physical restraint: reduction in legal fees
7. Reorganization of prison labor:
    a. minimum salary equal to national minimum wage
    b. social security for the family
    c. working papers upon release

      d. expansion of professional training during incarceration
8. Right of visitation and free correspondence
9. Right to decent medical and dental care
10. Right to appeal and defense of detainees in front of the prison administration (courtroom, conditional freedom, full pardons, etc.)
11. Right of association inside prisons (essential means for exercising the preceding claims).[25]

In the ninth issue, in September 1973, a twelfth point was added. It was featured on the last page with the title, "End to prison." An explanation was given for why it did not appear in the second issue: "Friends, buddies, comrades of all the slammers of this screwed society, the Committee of Prisoner Action almost forgot this point, since it seemed so obvious that it represents the crucial point of our opposition to imprisonment as a form of punishment."[26]

They added a completely consistent explanation: "Ultimately this twelfth point is in complete contradiction with the preceding ones. Those stem from simple humanity." The final verdict is conclusive: "Prison can't be fixed: it either destroys or is destroyed. We must decide which we prefer."[27]

The collective that broadcasts *L'Envolée*'s radio show and publishes the journal of the same name, put out a very exhaustive book in 2000, *Au pied du mur* [*Back Against the Wall*]. Its subtitle is explicit: "765 reasons to end all prisons." The introduction agrees: "The whole world seems to be in agreement, it is high time to destroy prisons."[28] Within the militant world, it is obvious to most of us. But one after another, the ministers of justice only speak of building new ones.

Back Against the Wall echoes Albert Jacquard: "We can't imagine a world without prisons without an end to money, the State, and all market relations."[29] This analysis is radical, but with equal deftness, it adds an element that places it in a direct line with CAP: "On this subject, the so-called revolutionary reactions of those who label any demand for improvement of conditions of detention as reform often miss the mark: each piece taken away from prison is a section of the wall that collapses."[30] This is why the struggle is systematic and perpetual: supporting prisoners in their demands and when they leave prison, but also striving ruthlessly for the deconstruction of the prison system.

The book cites Claude Lévi-Strauss, from *Tristes Tropiques*: "In most societies that we call primitive, this custom, 'prison,' would inspire a profound horror; in their eyes it would mark us with the same barbarity that we would be tempted to impute to them due to their symmetrically opposite customs."[31] It also cites Florence Bernault, author of the work, *Enfermement, prison et châtiments en Afrique, du XIXᵉ siècle à nos jours* [*Confinement, Prison and Punishments in Africa from the 19ᵗʰ century to the present*]: "In Cameroon, the Bassa clearly prove that these societies are marked by the absence of prisons. However, constraints exist. Thus, to immobilize a prisoner, they are made to wear wooden fetters on their shins: the ndi-keng."[32]

The book reports an event that happened in Chiapas after the Zapatista revolution. One man killed another during a bender and was sentenced to help the wife of his victim, as well as to tend her plot of land, in addition to his own personal duties. This is clearly an act of reparation.

Another striking example cited in *Backs Against the Wall*, quite far from all the clichés, is the Makhnovshchyna (Black Army), in its draft declaration of the revolutionary insurrectional army: "All the outdated forms of justice—court administration, revolutionary tribunals, repressive laws, police or militias, secret police, prison and all other old, counterproductive, useless junk—ought to disappear or be abolished from the first breath of free life, from the first steps of social, economic, free, living organization."[33]

We can end this world tour in the village of Ribeirao Bonito in the Amazons in 1975. Eduardo Galeano offers a very real image: "And, where prisons used to be, there is only a small pile of trash."[34]

Professor of philosophy at the University of Paris VIII Saint-Denis, Alain Brossat continues in the line of Catherine Baker, whom he cites on the back cover of his book, *Pour en finir avec les prisons* [*To End Prison*], published in 2001. This book is clearly more theoretical than pragmatic. The philosopher engages the debate on the level of principles. He attacks from the front: "The prison institution, as State apparatus, continues to stand out radically from other institutions, as a place and with a purpose completely geared towards death."[35] He refers to Kropotkin who, during a talk in Paris in 1887, said about prisons: "We cannot improve a prison. Besides some tiny irrelevant improvements, there is absolutely nothing to do but to demolish it."[36] Alain Brossat refers to Alexandre Jacob and his famous cry: "Down with prisons, all prisons!" And he also recalls Michel Foucault who, defending the position of the GIP, declared: "All we say is: no more prison at all."[37]

Freshly out of prison, Gabi Mouesca published *Prison@net. Journal d'un "longue peine"* [*Prison@net. Journal of a "long sentence"*]. He bluntly offers the lesson of his sixteen years of incarceration as a Basque political prisoner: "But there still remain many struggles to take on and to win in order to put an end to arbitrary power and carceral brutality . . . before permanently ending prison, with its outright abolition."[38]

There is another liberatory tendency in the work of architects. It has become clear over the course of years of architecture panels. We can look to Jacques Le Bihan, with *L'Espace carcéral* [*Carceral Space*], and Christian Moro, with *Une prison: un nouveau visage* [*A Prison: A New Face*] in 1992. We must also especially remember Augustin Rosenstiehl and Pierre Sartoux, who published *Construire l'abolition* [*Building Abolition*], in 2005. They asked Gabriel Mouesca, then president of OIP, to write a preface. Mouesca's conclusion is clear: "*Building Abolition* is a major contribution to the emergence of a better world. A world that cannot be made without throwing prisons, all of them, in the dustbin of history."[39]

Pierre and Augustin, as the preface-writer calls them, share the resources at their disposal as architects: "'To knock down' the prison compound is a first step towards the progressive abolition of prison that we aim for through successive stages of architectural deconstruction."[40] Another path they take is much more political: "The idea of self-management entails both the autonomous management by the incarcerated person and the collective management by the incarcerated population. This idea is an essential part of the project for the accountability of the incarcerated person."[41]

When we approach the question of abolition, people with good intentions ask us: "But how do you plan on achieving it?" It's one of the most sensible questions. It would be unthinkable to arrive at such an shift without having taken into account the people who are incarcerated themselves. The two architects make an argument that is as far-reaching ethically as it is politically: "A symbol of autonomy and of freedom, the grounds are a pilot test between punishment that takes away freedom and its abolition. It is a tool for people who are incarcerated and social workers with the goal of achieving autonomy over complete care. This tool is thus 'controlled' by the social workers who increase the amount of freedom for a person who is incarcerated according to a moral framework."[42] Once a re-entry and probation counselor comes to this point in their relation with the prisoner, they are looking at another stage in the deconstruction of prison. Rosenstiehl and Sartoux tell us: "Note in this regard that the old director of the Caen prison got rid of the solitary confinement block." Their final diagnosis leaves no room for excuses: "Prison today is poor people guarding poor people."[43]

As the subtitle "To end all prisons" shows, in 2009, *L'Envolée* used *Perpetual Sentences and Solitary Confinement* to expand on the truncated conclusion the Collective made in 2001. The testimonies of people who are incarcerated are overwhelming—they speak for themselves. The Resilient prisoner of Fresnes strikes a common refrain well known behind bars: "Torture can't be fixed, it must be abolished. Prison should cease to exist; it had its time, now it must die!"[44]

In *Brûler les prisons de l'apartheid* [*Burning the Prisons of Apartheid* (2012)], Natacha Filippi nods to Julius Van Daal's hallmark book: *Beau comme une prison qui brûle* [*As Beautiful as a Burning Prison*]. But Filippi does not only speak of South Africa. The prisoners that she met there asked her to speak about people incarcerated in France and their struggles. They wanted to know if they also burned their prisons.

Angela Davis published *Are Prisons Obsolete?* in 2003 (translated into French in 2014). The positions she articulates are a true update of the CAP's demands. Citing the movement of struggle against the prison industrial complex, she explains: "It calls for the abolition of the prison as the dominant mode of punishment but at the same time recognizes the need for genuine solidarity with the millions of men, women, and children who are behind bars."[45] It is also in the spirit of the French anti-prison movement not to separate the two battles. Angela Davis ask us not to oppose these two types of apparently distinct battles. She does not lack solutions—we will return to this further on. In any case, she gives us a necessary reminder: "Creating agendas of decarceration and broadly casting the net of alternatives helps us to do the ideological work of pulling apart the conceptual link between crime and punishment."[46]

With *Du droit à l'évasion* [*On the Right to Escape* (2014)], Jacques Colombat approaches the end of prison from another angle. He recalls the United Nations Economic and Social Council's text from 1948: "An open prison is a penitentiary establishment in which preventative measures against escape do not lie in material obstacles such as walls, locks, bars, or supplementary guards."[47] He writes sarcastically about a country in a unique situation in 1947: "Albania: no prisoners left. The seven prisons in Albania are completely empty after the final escape from the penitentiary where people sentenced to life were detained. Yesterday, the director of Albanian detention establishments declared to the Italian agency, ANSA: 'Albania is from now on the only country in the world to have no one incarcerated,' he complained."[48]

Political scientist Hélène Erlingsen-Creste worked as an advisor in the disciplinary committee at the remand home in Agen. She says, "The carceral system such as it is today is a clear failure for the person who is incarcerated just as much as it is for justice and society." She confirms: "The conclusion is clear: the more people we put in prison, the more they return to prison." She speaks honestly and directly: "Prison has demonstrated its limits and it is time to come to the present day and work towards other solutions."[49]

CHAPTER THREE

What Prison is Like

The general public doesn't have an intensely negative view of prison. The reasons for this are simple. First, widespread ignorance of the prison system persists. Films and reporting make no difference. The impact of the imagery is merely emotional and doesn't last. The media, like the rest of society, moves quickly. They only want to inundate us with big news stories. And so we romanticize fights, sodomy, the hole, madness, suicide . . . And without further ado, the reporting turns into a magazine article, a TV show, or a new traumatic event: an assault, an accident, floods, fire, or war . . .

New feelings replace the earlier ones. Comfort and a healthy amount of cynicism relegate the shocking views of prison to a recent past that has been totally overcome. A patient told me, "The way things are now, I can't tell the difference between movies and the news." Even if they are briefly interested, most people think, "I can't do anything about it. It's the way it is. I can't be so sensitive."

Laws were created to control human relations within the community. They aren't revolutionary. They only enshrine a particular society's way of functioning. That's why Montesquieu was able to say, "Truth is on this side of the Pyrenees; and beyond that, error." Laws aren't much bothered with psychology. Their purpose, in the form of duty, is instead socio-political.

Laws are almost always enacted mathematically. They enforce scales: this offense will be punished with a sentence of two to five years. This crime, with ten to twenty. But jurists don't wonder what happens after sentencing. Many of them make arguments with their ideas already decided: "Give him twenty years. He'll only serve ten." But that became untrue a long time ago, especially since the abolition of the death penalty. Most judges began to sentence more severely under the pretext that there was no longer a final punishment as a deterrent. Instead, for those who were in prison in 1963, another reality was established, one that was oppressive and permanent.

When Jean Foyer became Minister of Justice, parole began to be systematically denied. I studied this issue. People sentenced to twenty years no longer served ten years, but fourteen. Those with life sentences spent eighteen to twenty-two years inside . . . Obviously, today, with the burst of repressive and security laws, it's even worse!

The judge and the regular person are satisfied with the judicial system. It's only the stereotypes that make a splash. The dangerous mugger, the pedophile, or the angry hostage taker are no longer able to cause harm. They can no longer attack, rape, or rob us. Moreover, the collective imagination only imagines these types of people in prison. They don't know that 75 percent of people inside are ordinary people like them, or even poorer, who get caught up for minor offenses: a lack of permit, stealing a cellphone, pathetic scams and cons. What used to be called chicken thieves.

Sociological studies, especially Laurent Mucchielli's *Violences et insécurité* [*Violence and Insecurity*], show that feelings of insecurity are inversely proportionate to actual danger. Hence the deep relief when the police make an important arrest. It serves as a moral lesson: those who get arrested are automatically seen as villains, thieves, perverts, psychopaths, and killers.

No one—or nearly no one—asks about early morning raids and arrests any more: it's really shocking. In most cases, detention is inhumane, and involves the police officers taking turns harassing; stress; maybe a sandwich, swallowed in a hurry; lack of sleep; filth, since it's impossible to wash up. And, in certain cases, violence and beatings. Furthermore, there's the blackmailing of loved ones: "I'll detain your wife if you don't talk. Your kids will be taken away."

We have so much testimony along these lines. For example, Éric Sniady's *Entre quatre murs. Comment j'ai survécu trente ans dans l'enfer des prisons* [*Behind Bars: How I Survived Thirty Years in Prison Hell*]. It's an unquestionable testimony: "Putting a wife, or worse a mother in jail, seriously determines what happens next. In these situations, they'll almost always start talking." Éric gives an example: "They claim they can put her away as an accomplice and send her five-year old to child protective services."[1]

The first days in prison are nothing like the stories. It's a true devastation, called "prison shock." The prisoner is experiencing trauma. For over thirty years, this word has been fashionable. But it doesn't just occur through accidents or attacks. Everyone can be affected by it. The mind has no way to integrate such a series of brutal events.

The person ends up in a state of shock. They feel empty, completely removed from reality. They can't begin to analyze what has happened unless they've spent their lives in and out of prison.

Some people remain in a stunned state for a week. This process has been clearly described by psychologists and psychiatrists. The prison guards themselves realize it. They know that often during the first days of incarceration two accidents might occur: suicide or loss of reason (madness). Psychotic breaks are common in prison. This shows that the approach doesn't respond to the problem. And it only gets worse as the sentence progresses.

Here too Éric Sniady puts it bluntly: "Apart from those who were already ill, I encountered prisoners who started off with healthy minds, but who were lobotomized by prison over the years."[2] That's why, if they have orders, guards make regular rounds of the new arrivals. Most suicides take place just after arrest or sentencing.

We must always keep in mind that the suicide rate is seven times higher in prison than in society. Furthermore, in solitary, which they euphemistically call the "disciplinary unit," suicides increase sevenfold, which means that people take their own lives there forty-nine times more than in the free world! Therefore, we easily understand that when a relatively sane human being faces either flight into madness or death, a far healthier alternative still remains: escaping. This explains why the ordinary person is also fascinated by this kind of stunt.

We all remember Michel Vaujour's escape from la Santé when his wife came for him in a helicopter. In the depths of our psyche, though many of us get stuck on pain, illness, and death, the call to life remains strongest and makes us dream of love and freedom!

Based on the countless testimonies of formerly incarcerated people about imprisonment, we might wonder how it is possible that practically nothing about what it's like makes it to the general public. You only have to mention a few names in order to recognize that inescapable truths have been written about the prison system: Albertine Sazzarin, Maud Marin, Serge Livrozet, Claude Charmes, Roger Knobelspiess, Louis Perego, Charlie Bauer, Roland Agret, Jacques Lerouge, Philippe Maurice, Daniel Koehl, and more recently, Audrey Chenu, Vanessa Cosnefroy, Brigitte Brami, Éric Sniady...

The overall thrust of their work is clear. Prison doesn't solve the problem raised by delinquency and criminality—it makes it worse. It causes such suffering and such hatred that it can only lead to recidivism. It doesn't wipe out the poverty that it is supposed to deal with. It wipes out the poor. Loïc Wacquant shows this in *Les Prisons de la misère* [*Prisons of Poverty*]. Very often, prison kills.

The families of prisoners have insisted on reminding us that even outside, a spouse is also in prison, even if they haven't committed a crime ... Children are severely impacted. They even experience problems at school: "Your dad is in prison." To get to visitation, you have to make ridiculous journeys, especially when the incarcerated person is transferred to the other side of France. The spouse ends up in a state of precarity, because all of the expenses (rentals, kid's meals, travel) are their responsibility. In many cases, poverty is the result.

So what happens during these months and years inside? Catherine

Baker states in *Why Should We Punish?*: "No one wants to know about the abject environment of this closed-up world, about the hideous ugliness one must bear each minute, for months that seem like years, and years that become centuries."[3] Even though she's never been in prison as a prisoner, she still she knows the reality of prisons!

Michel Vaujour is someone who can best verify what she writes:

> After a moment, you begin to get caught in self-fulfilling cycles of thinking, and nothing can distract you. There are only the walls of the cell, which echo your obsessive thoughts back to you. Your thoughts "bounce" off the walls ... The time comes where you talk to yourself, a sentence here, a sentence there, coming out of your mouth in surprise ... and concern ... Silence–solitude=non-life. You are in an airtight container, locked up, and you no longer exist ... It gets to the point that you can no longer think, everything gets muddled. It all becomes confused in your head, you feel like your brain is numb. So you gaze into the void to try to find ... what you wanted to think about ... this void in your head ... Silence—thoughts—solitude—void—nothingness—non-being—"self" destruction—eternity.[4]

When you're free, you can't imagine such conditions. Or, at best, you might think these are the ideas of mentally ill people. But Michel Vaujour is an extremely intelligent person with sound mind. It's very difficult to write or talk about the confusion that comes when one sinks into madness. Especially after coming out of it.

Another person who escaped by helicopter, Serge Coutel, provides the same insight in *Back Against the Wall*: "When you know that you are going to do life, it's not just one day after another. No, each day you serve life as a whole with memories that look forward more and more the suffering to come. And this hardening of time crystallizes into a frosted glass ... And life becomes a disease ..."[5] These days, people inside talk about a slow death, which can be seen even more physically than mentally. All those who don't resist, either by involving themselves in sports, studies, or militancy, crumble bit by bit, and much faster than people of the same age on the outside. Those who vigorously perform serious physical exercise keep their health relatively intact, even if they are psychologically "broken."

The prisoner who undertakes or pursues education not only nurtures intellectual potential, but, at the cost of superhuman effort, succeeds in acquiring diplomas that will give them a chance to find a better level of work. The best example is Philippe Maurice who received a doctorate inside and became a university professor. He tells the story in a very interesting book, *De la haine à la vie* [*From Hate to Life*]. He is one of the great French medievalists.

The militant keeps up their rebellion and outrage, and they have a good chance at preserving their ability to resist. Pierre Campinchi, the last director of Caen central told me: "Rebels have the best chance of getting out." He got me out of a very bad situation. I had participated in three protest movements of resistant prisoners and I was writing a doctoral thesis on "emotional and sexual deprivation of incarcerated people," so I had been interviewing my incarcerated comrades. This had gotten me written up thirty-five times by the guards. As Pierre Campinchi took over, I was going to be transferred to the disciplinary center.

Let's go back to the nineteenth century... In *Are Prisons Obsolete?*, Angela Davis cites Charles Dickens's *American Notes*, which he wrote after his visit to Eastern Penitentiary in 1872:

> In its intention, I am well convinced that it is kind, humane, and meant for reformation; but I am persuaded that those who devised this system of Prison Discipline, and those benevolent gentlemen who carry it into execution, do not know what it is that they are doing. I believe that very few men are capable of estimating the immense amount of torture and agony that this dreadful punishment, prolonged for years, inflicts upon the sufferers ... I am only the more convinced that there is a depth of terrible endurance in it which none but the sufferers themselves can fathom, and

which no man has a right to inflict upon his fellow-creature. I hold this slow and daily tampering with the mysteries of the brain to be immeasurably worse than any torture of the body ... because its wounds are not upon the surface, and it extorts few cries that human ears can hear; therefore I the more denounce it, as a secret punishment which slumbering humanity is not roused up to stay.[6]

Maxime, who was an engineer for six years on "*Ras les murs*," served thirty-one years inside. One night, we had Lucien Léger on air—he had just gotten out after forty-one years! The anarchist militants were very impressed with his visible resistance to all these years of imprisonment. He still called himself an anarchist. Thus, it made total sense that he'd join up with like-minded militants when he got out. He participated in numerous discussions about prison, and it was astounding to see this man standing there, determined and very engaged. Yet, when Maxime saw him come into the studio, all skinny and stiff, with dark sunglasses and a Coca-Cola hat, he said out of the corner of his mouth (since in the studio you aren't supposed to speak): "I'm glad I got out after thirty-one years!" Lucien died two years after his release ... Maxime survived six years. They were both only in their sixties.

Prison is thus madness, suicide, escape, or death. Indisputably, we witness psychic, physical, or social destruction. Or all three. It's a world of violence.

In *Asylums*, Erving Goffman clearly explains the theoretical reasons. Totalitarianism and concentration camps contain a violence that gets attributed to guards and participants. But the most emotional and sensitive people don't resist the pressure of the institution, and are the first to explode, causing chain reactions. Since the asylum and the prison use repressive means, the matter gets resolved quickly, through the internal court and solitary confinement. This is without considering the settling of scores among guards, among incarcerated people, or between prisoners and guards.

Éric Sniady explains this with some striking examples: "A gang of eight guards entered my cell to punish me. I was severely beaten. They hit me with their hands and with their key rings. The ordeal lasted several minutes. At the end, they walked out, leaving me almost unconscious on the floor."[7] He gives another example: "Some [guards] get revenge on the sly, encouraging incarcerated people to attack other prisoners they already have trouble with. With my own eyes, I've seen four guys beating someone serving life, until he collapsed, unresponsive, on the ground. Face swollen and bloody, he seemed dead."[8] In the case of another brawl, Éric set the record straight. He and another person intervened. The two guards got scared and denied their part. Fascist thinking took over and it almost turned ugly: "In front of other incarcerated people, some screws promised to kill me if I didn't change my statement. Meanwhile, all of my mail was opened and thrown in the trash." The battle continued. Éric adds: "I heard that the newbies (*bleus*) asked other incarcerated people to put a contract out on my head. The methods of some screws are comparable to hoodlums.'" The situation grew more dangerous: "I was afraid that they'd plant contraband in my cell. That had already happened: some screws had no problem hiding cannabis or cellphones without the occupants knowing."[9] He got himself out of the situation by asking to be placed in the isolation wing. Giving one person power over others is the worst mistake. Hierarchy allows all kinds of abuses. Éric Sniady's conclusion is correct: "Penning people up only leads to suffering and desocialization."[10]

We must also take into account another aspect: health. Many nurses, doctors, and psychiatrists have written on this subject. Mental illness affects 30 percent of the prison population. In *Fresnes, histoires de fous* [*Fresnes Prison, Stories of the Mad*], journalist Catherine Herszberg describes unbelievable situations that do not belong in prison, but seems straight out of *One Flew Over the Cuckoo's Nest*.

But let's stay with the issue of general health, which includes all prisoners. We can cite a high-quality work that holds nothing back: *La Santé incarcérée* [*Incarcerated Health*] by Dr. Daniel Gonin, prison doctor and service coordinator of prison health for the Lyon region. His study, commissioned by the Minister of Justice, appeared in 1991, but was revised in the

2000s, the same time that another book was published by a prison doctor, Véronique Vasseur, from La Santé Prison.

Dr. Dominique Fauchet was a doctor in the isolation ward in Fresnes Prison. She wrote a memoir, which was published in full on the website *Ban public* (prison.eu.org). Obviously, her testimony isn't from the perspective of an incarcerated person, but its effect is devastating, since she confirms everything prisoners themselves describe. It also corroborates the answers to the questions I asked incarcerated people during my research for my dissertation. To be honest, it's not very surprising. But it's striking that the damage is the same despite the improvement of conditions of incarceration between 1960 and 2016 . . .

We must really listen to what Dominique Fauchet tells us: "To describe and discuss all of the situations where medical ethics are undermined during incarceration would exceed this present work. In fact, from admission to release, every moment of detention, every space in the prison provides opportunity for events that violate the dignity of people who are incarcerated, that threaten their physical and mental wellbeing and their autonomy. However, there are two places where prison restrictions disrupt our practice: the punishment block and the isolation ward."[11] All those involved speak of prison violence. Dr. Fauchet is no exception: "I quickly realized that no one would reach out a hand, literally nor figuratively, to this man. He was the victim of repeated harassment: rudeness, harsh words, insults, being ignored, refusal of small favors given others, and even intentional mistakes in medical treatment."

It's striking that this doctor's report contains all the same conditions we would encounter during incarceration regardless of whether we were a prisoner, professional, or militant. The people who reject or simply ignore these reports have their heads in the sand. In some cases, their denial is a symptom of a disturbing intellectual dishonesty. What is their real aim?

Our doctor mentions vision problems, intensified hearing, and the dullness of daily life: "The environment is so monotonous that sensory stimulation is reduced. People often complain about eye discomfort. Vision disorders are common in prison. The field of vision is limited to the cell walls, so there is no longer ability to see in the distance." Is mutilation part of the convicted person's sentence? Scores of incarcerated people have been condemning this inescapable aspect of double degradation since the beginning.

The doctor from Fresnes adds: "On the other hand, hearing is overly stimulated. The noise of locks, flushing, stereos, televisions, ringing of bars, the shouts of the staff (giving commands is done by yelling) and of other prisoners. The idea of pleasure is prohibited. Mental anguish affects every incarcerated person. However, it seems to be pushed to the extreme in solitary confinement." When it's impossible to see, attention gets focused on trying to prepare for events. What's going to happen? Is a guard coming? Will they catch me committing an infraction? Are they coming to find me for visitation, courthouse, exercise, or the court that is today hypocritically called "the disciplinary committee"? Free-floating anxiety attaches to sound, which is the only way potential danger manifests. The only sense capable of informing us is hearing.

In addition to matters of health, Dr. Fauchet remarks on the deeds of guards in prison space: "During cell searches, people's things are turned upside down, damaged, photos torn up . . . for safety!"

Éric Sniady mentions similar events: "As a result of the famous rebellion at Saint-Maur in 1987, uncooperative incarcerated people were transferred in their underwear. Their personal effects were split up among the screws, including precious jewelry. Though I didn't experience that episode, I had to endure the same inconveniences. The most infuriating was guards spilling a bottle of oil all over my stuff just for fun. Clearly it was their parting gift."[12]

In *Le Petit Paradis* [*Little Slice of Heaven* (1972)], Dr. Marcel Diennet catalogued all of the diseases he encountered at Fresnes prison: "There are so many illnesses caused by imprisonment: diabetes, tuberculosis, lung disease, and especially heart conditions. Then there are the surgical issues caused by prison, of course. All kinds of operations on 'swallowers' (people who ingest objects), suicide attempts, and finally all of the cases of infected lymph nodes, abscesses on the buttocks, anal fistulas caused by lack of hygiene . . . Ulcers of the dudodenal bulb are the most typical. Their causes are almost completely mental."[13]

On this subject, we can cite a cautionary example. Around 1965, at Caen Central, my friend Claudius, who was sentenced to ten years, started screaming in his cell in B block, after the doors were closed at 7pm. Every once in a while, we'd hear the commotion of a fight in the hall. Comrades started banging on the doors. The whole night, Claudius moaned and cried, expressing sharp pain. But the noise didn't stop until opening the next morning at 7am. We were told later that the night guards "weren't able" to get help! . . . My friend was operated on in the hospital. He had a perforated ulcer in the duodenum. When he came to, much later, the surgeon told him: "An hour later, and you would have been dead!"

Three decades later, Dr. Daniel Gonin's *Health in Prison*, reaches the same conclusion. Even though the law of January 18, 1994 moved responsibility for the health of incarcerated people from the Minister of Justice to the Minister of Health, we must stress that the situation is exactly the same today.

Abdel-Hafed Benotman experienced incarceration for many years. During his final time in prison, he became known as an exceptional writer of dazzling essays, novels, and plays. In the preface to his first work, *Les Forcenés [Maniacs]*, Robin Cook, a true visionary, writes of Benotman: "If I had to define the work of this writer, I would say that he rips out his heart in front of our eyes and lays it, still beating, on the table."[14] Specifically, during his two final incarcerations (2008/2011), Hafed had two myocardial infarctions. The first time, he waited six hours before being helped. The second time, twelve hours. On his final release, his heart only functioned at 25 percent. A few years later, in 2015, after having been one of the hosts of "*Ras les murs*" and having created the show "*L'Envolée*" with other militants, he died at the age of fifty-seven.

Dr. Daniel Gonin elaborates on this situation in *Health in Prison*. He lists the psychic and physical issues that he encountered in Saint-Paul prison in Lyon. Regarding visual impairments, he mentions Jeremy Bentham's cherished idea, the panopticon, which allows guards to see without being seen. The author offers this analysis: "In prison, there are those who see and those who are seen. Incarceration spells the death warrant for the exchange of glances that comes with talking."[15] The incarcerated person feels like they are potentially being watched at every moment. Over time, this creates a feeling of persecution, and thus paranoia. Solitude creates a deprivation of touch. The doctor quotes this haunting line: "What I miss the most is touch, skin against mine, the skin of a woman . . ." What ensues is a hyperesthesia that is understandable but unaccountable: "Since being incarcerated, I've been electric. When someone brushes against me or if I pass close to someone or something, I feel like a shock jolts through me." I know this phenomenon particularly well. Daniel Gonin's explanation is striking: "The outermost layer of skin acts now only as an alarm signal."[16] Alas, the disease doesn't end there.

The doctor dwells at length on teeth: "In prison, dental problems take over."[17] We all know that behind bars dentists are lacking, so as a result, toothaches without pain medicine are a part of daily life. And the most basic care is often replaced, after long waiting periods, with extractions straight out of wilderness medicine. I can't help mentioning Dr. Marcel Diennet's *Little Slice of Heaven*, which tells of another kind of procedure: "It took five men to hold him and he screamed during the whole operation, which lasted only five minutes."[18]

The digestive tract begins with the teeth, but it goes down much further. Daniel Gonin makes more observations: "On entering prison, digestive conditions are second only to dermatological conditions, on par with pulmonary and ear, nose, and throat conditions. But, while after six months skin conditions begin to diminish, problems with the digestive tract and respiratory tract start to grow, coming first after dental problems."

Since we previously mentioned "swallowers," we must explain what this means. Whether as a protest, or for self-mutilation, some incarcerated people consume objects that are as unexpected as they are harmful. The author gives us a long list: "All kinds of objects are swallowed by incarcerated people: while making them, they swallow clothespin springs, also bolts, fork and spoon handles, pieces of beer cans, ballpoint pens, and even plastic bucket handles. The most remarkable are razor blades."[19] Of course, sometimes these acts are boasted about. Often, they remain unexplained. Prisoners reach such a level of suffering that they don't need any more reasons for self-harm. They show the state of desperation they have reached. The doctor uses a psychoanalytical interpretation to try to understand something he heard from one incarcerated person: "He is now nothing but a pipe without connection to the living. The omnivore, who maintains vital relationships of nourishment with the animal and vegetable worlds, no longer exists. He languishes in an existence of nothingness, stiffened by the mineral or metal he incorporates. He has become the stone, the fire, the glass, and plastic inside him. He is his own prison wall."[20]

Without claiming to cover everything, we will end this chapter on health in prison with skin. Daniel Gonin reframes the challenges: "Dermatological therapy clearly follows far behind psychotropic drugs, but competes for second or third place with antibiotics and analgesics."[21] This doesn't mean that this area is spared: "On the incarcerated person's skin all stages of boils develop. . . Eczema covers the legs even of young people who have 'been through it,' allowing to discover sometimes long-established ulcers. After admission into prison, incarcerated people are brought suffocating with angioedema where widespread swelling has also constricted their respiratory tracts. Rashes on irregular and abnormal skin areas appear and disappear as a result of treatment with antihistamines or with cortisone compounds."[22] The doctor's assessment makes one wonder: "We might say that skin displays the stress, anxiety, discomfort of arraignment and incarceration, becoming the wall of imprisonment as such. Thus, an individual wall of incarceration is permanently built. The hide is now tanned inside and out."[23]

CHAPTER FOUR

Sex and Prison

If we are talking about health, we can't ignore feelings, emotions, affects, and sexuality. Of course, this is not a great era in which to address these issues. During the 1990s, an initial return of the moral order took place in our societies due to the outbreak of HIV, and today a second return, more marginal but also more violent, is the pseudo-religious response to "radical Islamists."

It is difficult to deal with sensitive matters that are deep and essentially human in a world riven by an emotional plague, as Wilhelm Reich described it. We are far from a sexual revolution! In society, we hear warnings of withdrawing into distinct, parochial communities; of moralism and prudery; of incredible hypocrisy; of latent hostility set to explode at any moment; and finally, as a result, of a widespread fear quickly rising to the level of terror.

Accordingly, the champions of security control the conversation. The press approaches them saying, "Reassure us. We are scared to death. Tell us that you will do something for us." The response comes ominously: "Be calm. I'm here to protect you. Vote for me. I will pass extreme security measures."

In 1965, when I began my doctoral thesis, "The psychological effects of emotional and sexual deprivation on the incarcerated person," despite the prohibition by the director of Caen Central, it was clearly a serious issue.

The Abolition of Prison

According to the ten interviews of the pilot survey amongst my comrades, I discovered the echo of what I knew so well myself: an internal hell, immense suffering, burning frustration, physical torture, psychological damage due to rage, anger, fury, hatred, and rebellion.

Moreover, I have needed to amend my questions since the discussion is so sensitive. Prisoners talk to me because I am a "hoodlum," that is someone who doesn't snitch or inform. But there is a rule of the "joint" that I don't follow: not only do I talk with gay men, but I also talk with sexual offenders, the infamous *"pointeurs"* [prison slang for sex offender]. I chose interviewees through a principle of random sampling from these two categories ("hoodlums" and *"pointeur")* so that in the main survey of around fifty incarcerated people, there were twenty from cell block B, twenty from Improvement (cell block C) and ten, later, on day parole. I met the latter in town, in Caen, when I myself was on conditional release in 1968 and 1969.

There's no need to go over everything the prisoners told me during this research. Since that time, it has been repeated in full in books, articles, debates, panels, radio and even television shows.

The Punishment of Sex (La Guillotine du sexe) started a debate with its first edition in 1978, and reprints in 1992 and 1998. Other authors came to support the struggle, especially Alain Monnereau, with *Prison Castration (La Castration pénitentiaire)* in 1986, and Arnaud Gaillard, with *Sexuality in Prison (La Sexualité en prison)* in 2009. Starting in 1971, along with Michel Foucault, as part of the Prison Information Group, we sent our first message in a bottle, the pamphlet *The Intolerable Ones (Les Intolérables)*, which tackles issues like "Model Prison: Fleury-Mérogis" and "Prison Suicides." In the Prisoner Action Committee, we published a special issue of the *Prisoner Journal* (no. 38, July 1976): "The emotional life and sexuality of prisoners." In 1981, the French prisoner union demanded intimate visits in the Saint-Paul de Lyon prison. In 1985, this demand would be made again by the French Prisoner Labor Organization (ASPF [l'Association syndicale des prisonniers de France]), which included 1,700 members of the 42,000 total incarcerated population of the time.

Meanwhile, Robert Badinter, Minister of Justice, formed a committee on "Prison Architecture," whose aim was to provide the concept of a forward-looking institution in Mauzac, in the Dordogne region. This was in 1984 and I was among the members. We turned in our report in April 1985. I was tasked by the Minister of Justice with interviewing prisoners, so I traveled to Fresnes, to the Jacques-Cartier de Rennes jail, to the Rennes Women's Detention Center, to the Muret Detention Center near Toulouse, and to the Caen Detention Center. We merely stated the obvious . . . All of the responses were in favor of the emotional and sexual relations that would come with intimate visits. However, at Fresnes, a more political objection was made: "We wouldn't want that to become a means of blackmail . . ."

The new prison in Mauzac opened in September 1986. It was built with different wings, allowing highly flexible connections between the workshops and the activity spaces. In addition, incarcerated people would be able to work outside the institution. Above all, in the visiting rooms, there would be conjugal rooms, including a couch, a fridge, a table, and armchairs . . . But the Right came into power and turned its back on the committee's suggestions.

Supported by the new Minister of Justice, Albin Chalandon, the new director of prison administration, Arsène Lux, didn't follow our recommendation to open the conjugal rooms. He turned them into regular visiting rooms. This showed a reactionary, sadistic, and completely irresponsible way of thinking.

Fortunately, the director of Mauzac took the committee's wishes into account. The visiting rooms had a windowed area that wasn't closed off with curtains, as had been planned for the conjugal rooms. It was the worst kind of meanness! No problem! The director gave the overseers instructions: "When you are at the visiting rooms, don't look inside. Look in the air or on the ground. But not inside." From September 1986 to June 1989, eight visiting room babies were born. Of course, the next director reverted to the rightwing and repressive policy.

In 1989, however, Gilbert Bonnemaison submitted a report to the prison administration; he had been asked to look at how the emotional and sexual relationships of incarcerated people were maintained in long-sentence institutions. In 1995, the administration received a final report from a new working group, which concluded that there was an urgent need to establish what would be called family visit units (UVF—*les unités de visites familiales*).

Shortly after, in 1997, two hundred incarcerated people at Bois-d'Arcy delivered a platform of demands to the prison director. They demanded the removal of the partitions in the visiting room, the increase of the length of visit to forty-five minutes instead of thirty, and the fogging of the cubicle windows in order to allow more intimacy during the visit. A few months later, the prisoners of Moulins-Yzeure sent a "Manifesto for the Establishment of Open Visiting Rooms" to the new Minister of Justice, Élisabeth Guigoux.

This led to comments from the judge Jean Favard in the journal *Dedans Dehors* [*Inside Outside*], published by the OIP, in May 1998: "The first, most urgent step consists in setting up family visiting rooms for those who are suffering the most serious psychological harm. In due course, we will have to go all the way with the thinking that imprisonment is only detention and nothing else."[1] It is notable that an "upstanding" person like Jean Favard, a pillar of French justice, clearly references the results of emotional and sexual deprivation for the incarcerated person. Alluding to Valéry Giscard d'Estaing's famous remark that "prison should only be the loss of liberty," he brings us to the substance of the debate. The UVF are nothing more than one of the elements of deconstructing prison. The real issue is imprisonment. Between the intimate visit and the abolition of prison, what should we prioritize?

There are a number of countries that have found solutions to the issue of sexuality behind bars: Sweden, Canada, Denmark, Finland, Norway, the Netherlands, the Republic of Moldova, Brazil, Mexico, India, Honduras, Puerto Rico, Poland, Yugoslavia, Russia, and some former-USSR countries.

Family visit units were only established in France in 2003. The stay in the UVF lasts between six and forty-eight hours. The UVF can be renewed after three months. Once a year, it is possible for the visit to last up to seventy-two hours. The visits take place in living quarters outside the space of detention, reproducing aspects of the couple's free life. The parent can come with or without children. It should be noted that it is a space without a formal mechanism of surveillance. But it isn't always a question of sex. The prisoner can be visited by a father, mother, or brother, too.

The experiment was undertaken at three institutions: the Rennes Women's Detention Center, which made me particularly happy; the Poissy Central; and the prison center on the Isle of Rhé. Ever since, each time a new prison is built, UVF are provided. Thus, today, we have dozens of them in the French prison establishment.

Should we consider what we have gained? Is the problem solved? Do we need to keep setting up family visit units? Today there is an open debate on this. The UVF are far from solving the problem of emotional life and sexuality in prison. They only benefit a small part of the prison population. Most people continue to languish in the greatest misery in this regard.

We can't forget that the UVF are only intended for those who can't benefit from leave. Thus the whole problem is: why this lack of leave permission? The reasons don't change—they are well known. The individual is not far enough along in the sentence. For example, once they reach half of their sentence, they have the right to request conditional release. Thus, they can also apply for leave. But it can be refused because it is premature or because the person can't provide a guarantee of return, place, family, psychological maturity, or recognized potential for re-entry . . . The parole board makes the decision and isn't truly accountable.

In *Sexuality and Prison*, Arnaud Gaillard tells us: "In Val de Rueil in 2007, out of 430 people permitted to take leave, only 71 incarcerated people have received permission."[2] Where does that leave the others? Even if the UVFs exist, only a portion of those not allowed leave get to use them. For a simple reason: the prison doesn't have enough studios or apartments to permit all of the requests.

Another issue is discreetly ignored. Receiving loved ones is the prisoner's financial burden. This began from good intentions: the individual should be autonomous and responsible. But this disregards the economic reality of prison. A number of incarcerated people don't have sufficient means, and even without being completely destitute, they don't have the means to buy supplies from the commissary for one or two close people, in addition to themselves, for one or two days. The UVF are thus closed to them, which creates further discrimination.

One of the main focuses of the debate currently taking place about priorities pits the UVF against leave. The threat of the intimate visit is to allow the administration and people with good intentions to reassure themselves cheaply: "We have improved the conditions of imprisonment. We don't need to try to go further. Prison has been humanized. We can even indefinitely extend sentences..."

The issue isn't to decide what the correct answer is. But the argument that it's only important to focus on leave, alternative sentences, "outside work," or day parole gets stuck in a similar logic. The error is to prefer one method over another. Increasing the number of UVF brings some prisoners an emotional and psychological relief; it gives them a chance to be less frustrated, upset, and imbalanced, and it will be less difficult for them to re-enter upon release. But, on a national level, this progress only takes place at a slow trickle and can't answer the real problem, and thus doesn't deserve to be considered revolutionary.

Getting a leave provides even more to the prisoner, with regard to real life. The prisoner is no longer watched. They have to figure it all out themselves. They get around, navigate, travel without guards opening and closing the doors for them. They have to go shopping themselves. Wherever they go, they have to face managing a room, a studio, an apartment, or a house. Even if they go to someone else's home. They meet lots of people, breathe free air, rediscover city traffic and the stress of public transport. Without a doubt, it's stressful, but so much more encouraging.

Thus we can favor leaves over UVF, but the real issue is knowing where the administration stands. Is justice always on the side of total repression, resulting in overpopulated prisons with soaring inflation? Are we always going to be under the threat of Islamist terrorists? Do we have the means to identify them and stop them, or even help them transform?

Do the players in our society spend their time in fear and thus in repression? Do they listen to thinkers like the Muslim philosopher Abdenour Bidar? He reminds us that it is a mistake to spend your time condemning enemies and the threat they pose to us. Doing so maintains our fear, paralyzes us, and stops us from acting. It is one hundred times more preferable to engage, to go towards those who are different than us and to establish means for ongoing encounters.

From the angle of prison abolition, it is always preferable to increase the ways to deconstruct prison. To do this, we can never ignore the balance and health of incarcerated people. Though we can't prepare them for release by destroying them, we also must keep our eyes on the interest of the collective. What do we learn from the improvement of conditions of detention and alternatives to incarceration? There are always lower recidivism rates ...

In her book *Sexualité incarcérée* [*Incarcerated Sexuality* (2015)], Nina Califano gives an unforgiving assessment of the current situation demonstrated by her research: "If today, in France, visits without surveillance are allowed in the context of family visit units, which indirectly allow incarcerated people to have sexual relations with their partner in decent conditions, this progress must be put into perspective in light of the limited number of incarcerated people who benefit from this system, and we must emphasize that the problem of sexuality in prison remains unchanged for most incarcerated people."[3]

CHAPTER FIVE

No Integration, No Re-Entry

The current discussion about prison within the justice system and prison administration links exclusion and re-entry. From the beginning, imprisonment had the single aim of removing disruptive, dangerous, mad, or criminal individuals from society. As the discussion aimed to be increasingly humane, it became clear that one day the prisoners would have to be released. The goal wasn't to keep them for life, nor was it to make them die.

But the decision makers, the politicians and philosophers, discovered that prison has devastating effects on the human psyche. Thus there has been research into reformation, rehabilitation, isolation, and community life. Little by little, a way of thinking has developed that focuses on helping the incarcerated person, to prepare them for release, and even to offer ways for them to take control over their own re-entry.

One of the best examples is what was called "prison reform," in 1945. Politicians who were imprisoned during the war of 1939–1945 became aware of the desocialization caused by years in prison. Therefore they created the progressive system. Sentences would be carried out in four phases. The first was isolation, which allowed observation of the prisoner for a year, nine or six months, depending on the institution and era. This was called block A or T1. The second period consisted of community life (activities, sports, work), all while living in an individual cell. The majority of the sentence would be carried out in this way. Once the incarcerated person reached the middle of their sentence and could be recommended for provisional release, they were able to move to block T3, or Improvement. The fourth phase was day parole. The central prisons were used for pilot experiments, including Caen, Melun, and Muret. A few others followed suit. Thus, they were no longer called central prisons, but detention centers.

These detention centers gave hope to those who benefited from the changes. Group living in block B went towards socialization and thus re-entry. At Caen, moving from block B to Improvement allowed one to prepare and eat a communal meal. Cells were open the whole day and didn't have bars. However the availability of four teachers for a population of 300–400 incarcerated people from the whole institution was more theoretical than actual. One of them told me: "I have a hundred students, but I can only work with thirty."

From 1960 to 1970, it was clear that the most sought after objective was re-entry. In the 1970s, with the anti-prison movements, this discourse was fiercely challenged: "It is ridiculous to talk about reintegration for people who, for the most part, have never been integrated at all." This analysis was very political. During this time, under the influence of Michel Foucault, Serge Livrozet, and CAP, it was often repeated that three-quarters of criminals were incarcerated for economic reasons. They were thus considered political prisoners. From 1985 on, following the ASPF, they were called social prisoners. But it was the same line of thought. The term reintegration was completely discredited, even if the prison administration persisted stubbornly to use it.

Today, it's the same. When we consider the prison population, it's obvious that we mostly find poor, precarious, unemployed, marginalized, undocumented people who have committed no offense; we find drug users, and all the poverty created by capitalist society. But the term reintegration remains strongly defended by a great number of professionals, even if it is completely rejected by militants and all of those who are really politicized.

It is obvious that a large percentage of the criminals who make up the standard type of incarceration have never been integrated in the first place.

What shall we then think of the double mission of prison: to protect society and prepare re-entry? In *A World Without Prison*, Albert Jacquard asks the perennial question: "The fundamental debate is over the purpose of the institution: is its first role to protect society by preventing harm, or to transform troublemakers into good citizens?"[1] The geneticist didn't have the slightest illusion: "There have hardly been areas where hypocrisy has been and remains as profound. All of the claims put rehabilitation above protecting society, but all of the actual policies prioritize protection."[2]

We can approach this discussion from a moral, psychological, sociological, or political perspective. It might be reassuring for public opinion to put criminals in prison. But it is a miscalculation; almost all of them wind up being released. And the worse they were treated, the more likely they are to go back in.

One of the claims we find most often among the researchers, statisticians, and demographers, is that incarceration only protects us very briefly. It has a perverse double effect on the length of imprisonment. Albert Jacquard states it quite clearly: "The percentage of recidivism testifies to the danger of the current practices: repeat offenders represent almost two-thirds of incarcerated people."[3]

In *Why Must We Punish?*, Catherine Baker discusses the International Conference on Penal Abolition: "The International Conference on Penal Abolition (ICOPA) meets every two years around the world." She tells us that in 1987, the ICOPA claimed that "there was no use fighting against prison as long as the prison system and the will to punish lasts."[4] Just like Albert Jacquard, she concludes quite logically that prison is a failure. In the long run, it achieves the opposite effect of what it claims: it increases delinquency and criminality through recidivism. It is thus time to change the system. At the end of *In Place of Prisons*, Dennie Briggs hammers out a truth that could prove to be prophetic: "We must be truly ready to change, and to acknowledge that this will make those who cannot adapt to change obsolete—like the two hundred men still on duty in the empty prisons of Massachusetts."[5]

In *Lost Causes: Must We Eliminate Prison?* [2002], Dominique Vernier gives a basic example, as related by Jacques Léauté from the American Osborne: "To prepare a return to freedom from prison is equivalent to training for a run by staying in bed for weeks."[6] For release not to be followed quickly by deprivation, isolation, failure, and relapse, many social processes would need to be radically transformed. In line with this, the journalist challenges us: "What risks is society ready to take so that human beings in violation of the law at some point are able to resume their place in society?"[7]

Ministers and senators provided many responses in the 2000 report, *Prisons, une humiliation pour la République* [*Prisons: An Embarrassment to the Republic*]. For example, the ministers ask: "When the mere use of drugs is subject to a sentence of one year imprisonment, how are we supposed to understand the meaning of this penalty under these conditions?"[8]

This is a discussion we find in the Ministry's report, *La France face à ses prisons* [*France's Response to Prisons*], but in the senatorial report, *Prisons: An Embarrassment to the Republic*, they don't bother with political double-speak: "The place for drug users as such is not prison. The mere consumption of drugs should not entail sentences of imprisonment."

The response is radical. If social abandonment isn't programmatic, there is no longer need for reintegration. Dominique Vernier doesn't overlook an even clearer assertion made by the senators regarding non-citizens incarcerated because they don't have legal entry: "Most of this population doesn't belong in prison, with the exception of course of those who are convicted, specifically for long sentences, as terrorists."[9]

Many other defendants could also avoid prison: mentally ill people, elderly people, pregnant women and everyone with children, minors, all of those with serious illnesses, and those who are physically disabled. They would always benefit from appropriate alternatives and not being cut off from society. And therefore they would not need to be reintegrated.

If we approach the question of incarceration more broadly, we come back to Loïc Wacquant's book, *Prisons of Poverty*:

> One must add to this labor-market impact the destabilizing effects of incarceration on the populations and places most directly put under penal control: the stigmatization and the sense of indignity that it carries; the interruption of educational, marital, and occupational trajectories; the destabilization of families and the amputation of social networks; the crystallization of a "culture of resistance" and even defiance of authority in the dispossessed districts where imprisonment is becoming a routine occurrence, even a normal stage in the life course of lower-class young men; and the whole train of pathologies, suffering, and (inter)personal violence commonly associated with passage through the carceral institution.[10]

Politicians operate in a completely inconsistent way. A way that even seems bipolar. After all of the critiques of prison made by ministers and senators, it might have seemed that the State was finally going to take part in the anti-prison struggle: questioning prison, improvement of conditions of detention, increasing alternatives to incarceration ... Then, in 2007, Nicolas Sarkozy became president of the Republic, which was a 180-degree turn towards repression: enhanced security measures in every news story; the harshest laws possible, exponential growth of the prison population, a return to prison construction. He was confident that he would succeed in eradicating the needy and in reassuring the privileged.

In 1985's *L'Année sociologique*, Bruno Aubusson de Cavarlay wrote an article titled *"Hommes, peines et infractions"* ["People, Sentences, and Violations"], in which he said definitively: "Fines are for the bourgeois and petit-bourgeois; incarceration with probation is for the masses; unconditional incarceration is for the underclass."[11]

In 2013, Gabi Mouesca did an interview with the publication *Alternative libertaire* [Anarchist Alternative], while he was the president of the OIP, where he said powerfully: "Prison is punishment of the poor. If we tackled the roots of poverty, the determinants of injustice, and inequalities, we would have no more prisons."[12]

In the July/August 1972 edition of the magazine *Esprit*, Jean-Marie Domenach, a member of GIP, said, "Contrary to the declared goal of the lawmakers, the most certain effect of prison is to make incarcerated people lose hope and to lead them to recidivism."[13] Kropotkin pushes this reasoning to its conclusion: "If one day it were decided that no punishment be inflicted on murderers, indeed it is very likely there would be a fall in the number of cases involving recidivists, brutalized in the prisons."[14] It is amazing that Kropotkin could write that in 1885. He was a visionary! Pronouncements like this are what made him so disruptive. We are all the more aware of this point today, when we have mediation, reparation, and meetings between offenders and victims.

Another rebel, Éric Sniady, attests to this truth: "Throwing someone into the hole for decades makes no sense. That will only ruin and dehumanize them. After forty years, in what state will this person come back out? Better not to even think about it . . ."[15] But let's actually think about it. We can't forget Lucien Léger . . .[16]

In *Incarcerated Sexuality*, Nina Califano cites the architect Christian Demonchy: "We claim we are resocializing people while forcing them into the worst social life imaginable."[17] She enumerates several factors that seem to explain this situation: "Many offenders have shown that prison desocializes through isolation, deprivation, subjugation, and continuous infantilization."[18] Thus she makes the unequivocal conclusion that, "It's another one of the many paradoxes of prison, to aim to resocialize people while stripping them of other people, of shared sexuality, and reducing social relations to almost nothing."[19]

In *Sexuality and Prison*, Arnaud Gaillard elaborates the same analysis: "The body withers away, the relationship with others makes outside society seem like an unknown land."[20] He goes on, "In this way, the combination of incarceration and warping of relations with others through processes of continuous deprivation creates an especially desocializing environment.

Prison makes people unlearn how to live with others by heightening defense mechanisms and violence ..." And further: "Whether it's violence against oneself, against others, or creating over time an expertly maintained culture of hostility towards the institution and the society that authorizes it, prison most often locks up delinquents and releases anti-social monsters."[21]

These testimonies and studies speak for themselves. We only need to mention the recidivism figures in order to support what they describe. It is not a matter of quibbling or haggling over variables of 5 or 10 percent. If we look at a range from 1970 to today, recidivism of people incarcerated for the first time hovers around 50 percent. Depending on the region and time period, it goes higher, sometimes up to 60 percent. The least we can say about this is that this fact doesn't make the case for incarceration. Are there businesses that could last with failure rates of 50 percent and higher? Well, what are standards for prison as an institution?

When we discuss people who have been incarcerated multiple times, the rate of return exceeds 70 percent, a fact that supports the popular belief that prison is the university of crime. When I facilitated support groups at the Bois-d'Arcy prison from 1986 to 2002, I knew of juveniles who simply went in and out of prison. It's a common occurrence. These young people go back in at a rate of 90 percent. Every social worker reports similar situations in juvenile wings, whether in Osny, Fleury-Mérogis, or any other institution.

Researchers, statisticians, and demographers agree on the numbers. In his publications, Pierre-Victor Tournier, who no one would suspect of laxness, comprehensively highlights the fact that alternatives result in lower recidivism numbers than prison time. When time comes for release, conditional release always proves to be more beneficial than "dry release" (release without support)—of course that is not considering sentence reductions. Accommodations, outside work, and day parole always lead to better results spending the whole time behind bars ...

A comprehensive reappraisal of the management of delinquency and criminality is needed. The fact that France has been condemned by Europe doesn't seem to bother politicians on the left or right too much. But it is becoming urgent and essential that politicians, professionals, militants, and researchers join together to create a new justice system.

Many other types already exist. It's time to look at what happens elsewhere. An example that demands our lingering attention is the community system of security, justice, and reeducation in the State of Guerrero, as an extra-state institution in Mexico.

CHAPTER SIX

Alternatives to Incarceration

The Forerunners

Madness, suicide, and escape are the reactions to a life of agony. You'd have to be seriously indifferent to not understand this. Once things reach this point, it's obviously a red flag. With so many people between life and death, it's not an individual problem. This is a call to community, social, and political aid. Who will take responsibility?

The smallest lesson we can draw is that our criminal justice system doesn't solve the problem it is tasked with. It reacts with a system of traps and dungeons, which is a short term strategy. We won't go over everything that has been said about its failure. Instead, we wonder if we can't seriously take inspiration from all of those who have written on this subject, Alain Brossat, Angela Davis, and so many others . . .

The dead end of prison must be questioned on its very premises. The fact that it doesn't achieve significant results should be enough for us to leave it behind. It is time to move towards something else. We know that it addresses a problem without having the means to do so. It is imperative to shift gears, to adopt another way of thinking. Anarchist theorists have paved the way; Kropotkin spent his life demonstrating that the best treatment for crime is freedom and community.

The Abolition of Prison

For years, Gabi Mouesca has been saying that if poverty disappeared from society, prison would essentially have no more reason to exist. Loïc Wacquant is right to call them "prisons of poverty." Victor Hugo was the first to say that for every school we open, we could close a prison. All of these elements combined make up the outlines of a revolutionary theory. If we want a true transformation of justice in our societies, we will not get there by tinkering and patching things up.

We must begin thinking from the premise of the elimination of prison. We can only share Catherine Baker's and Alain Brossat's perspectives. Anarchist theories give us convincing views. Prison can only be removed if society is radically transformed. Profit, competition, and money must cease to rule the world. Albert Jacquard states explicitly, "A society without prisons can only be a society that has no need for prisons."[1]

The way a social group operates can be so evolved that it is no longer necessary to have recourse to repression, violence, and imprisonment. Around the world, there have been successful experiments. One of the most striking examples of our time is the community of Indigenous villages of Guerrero that dispensed with the prisons of the Mexican state.

But we must remember other regions. We won't find any prisons in the Yucatan, in the southeastern Gulf of Mexico. Similarly, the village of Kakabila in Nicaragua, on the Caribbean coast, works through general assembly. Nearly everything is decided through direct democracy. Conflicts are handled collectively. No need for court or jail. It's the same for Barbuda, an island in the Lesser Antilles.

In New Caledonia, tribes didn't use closed spaces to punish people who didn't follow the rules. It was France that established Camp-Est (East Camp) on the main island, le Caillou, replicating the worst of its secular model ... In the conflicts of the Kanak people, everything is handled through traditional justice. Following the assassination of Jean-Marie Tjibaou, years of mediation were needed between the tribe of the killer and that of the victim to reach a compromise that allowed for healing. Furthermore, the youth in Île de Maré, whom I encountered in 2004 during a conference on adolescence, described to me the extent to which they were wedged between tribal justice and French justice. For the same thing, they were judged twice.

Of course, the automatic response is that societies without prisons can only exist because they are small-scale. But it is not ridiculous to envision local solutions fitting to a village or neighborhood. The increasing number of small-scale experiments might end up preempting the big carceral capitals. The vast amount of alternatives to incarceration might end up making the most overcrowded prison obsolete.

But this assumes that politicians, with the help of militants, organizations, and businesses, agree to sponsor pilot experiments that are revolutionary, respectful of the person and of common freedom. Many already exist; we can identify several. It is true that this type of commitment is tiring, perhaps exhausting, which explains why these innovations so often vanish once their founders stop working. If they had a strong enough support network and a secure financial base, they could last much longer, provided that turnover is covered.

This is where we are with our discussions, since a significant part of the population takes no interest in prison—except the loved ones of those inside. Just the opposite, for a certain part of the population, who think the tougher we are on convicts, the better. Many are still stuck on justice as vengeance, and we would like to develop a timeline of alternatives to incarceration for this inevitable portion of the public. The timeline would mean the changes could be applied without violence and without total societal upheaval, but with a success that is clearly visible to everyone. The alternatives allow for significant savings and a substantial decline in the rate of recidivism.

In a world where fear rules and security is its political cure, it is not even possible to make more security-based proposals.

Let's begin with Maxwell Jones, starting in 1941. This psychiatrist treated patients at Mill Hill, which was connected to Maudsley Hospital in the outskirts of London. In 1944, he conducted role-playing with the residents, following the example of Moreno, the founder of psychodrama. An advocate of social psychiatry, Jones came to conceptualize the therapeutic community, of which he is considered the father.

With patients diagnosed as psychopaths, maladjusted, antisocial, or simply delinquent, this psychiatrist developed an alternative. From 1947 to 1959, he brought it to Baltimore Hospital, in the suburbs of London. At first, the therapeutic community could include up to one hundred beds. It was only later that it was implemented in smaller locations. In 1962, Maxwell Jones was able to establish his method at the scale of four hundred patients, at the Dingleton hospital in Scotland, sixty kilometers from Edinburgh.

Dr. Jones left the UK in 1969 for the US, where he met the sociologist Douglas Grant and the psychologist Dennie Briggs. Though he had a psychoanalytic background, he was especially interested in the social aspects of treating mentally ill people and delinquents. This is how he influenced the two Americans.

In his view, imprisonment was a problem, whether it was carceral or psychiatric. Opening the doors enabled the opening of the mind. Dr. Paul Sivadon and Dr. Roger Gentis have done much to spread Maxwell Jones's ideas. We must note that Franco Basaglia, Ronald Laing, and David Cooper have likewise greatly contributed to the development of therapeutic communities.

With Joseph Berke, Laing and Cooper founded Kingsley Hall in 1965. This incredible adventure lasted until 1969, and led to the book *Journey Through Madness*, told by the patient Mary Barnes and her psychiatrist Berke. In ward 21, from 1962 to 1966, David Cooper conducted an experiment faithful to Maxwell Jones's thinking but within a big psychiatric hospital.

In his book, *In Place of Prisons*, Dennie Briggs notes: "The infection spread and soon Doug Grant provided the opportunity and the direction for a similar experiment to take place at one of the Californian prisons. A therapeutic community similar to the one at Henderson Hospital was set up. Maxwell Jones, on a Commonwealth visiting professorship in California, provided expert guidance."[2] The sociologist Douglas Grant believed that we shouldn't leave prisoners and prison staff to stagnate behind bars. Instead, "Grant's idea was that prisoners and staff could collaborate and learn from studying themselves and their surroundings rather than just being locked away."[3] Maxwell Jones had the brilliant idea of using marginalized and anti-social people to help their fellows develop social and psychoanalytic understanding. Douglas Grant and Dennie Briggs were going to help them take advantage of this.

The experiment was named "The New Careers Development Project." The main idea of the founders, faithful to Jones, was to call on former offenders to look after the young people in the new program. Behind this innovation lay an even more radical project: "The question must be faced squarely ... of how to halt the expansion of large institutions and how to run down those already in existence."[4] We can readily imagine that such innovators broke with the dominant ideology. The idea of guilt was foreign to their philosophy. With Maxwell Jones, we begin from a new foundation: "Abandoning traditional concepts of punishment, the therapeutic community saw all acts of delinquency as commentary."[5]

The project began in 1971 with one thousand incarcerated people held in the Massachusetts juvenile prison for people younger than seventeen years old. Around three hundred were placed in halfway houses, around three hundred were placed in ordinary housing, and around three hundred in foster families. In 1973, none of them remained in prison. The majority were on conditional release, others in collective programs without lodging, and still others in judicial diversion, that is, a suspended sentence. This meant that incarceration was replaced with lodgings, social programs, and greater conditional release. Each treatment was individual, with doctors, psychologists, social workers, lawyers, and former offenders taking part. They used pedagogical, psychological, and social methods for a duration of two years. The results met the expectations of Douglas Grant and Dennie Briggs. The baseline population of the Massachusetts prison had a recidivism rate of 45 percent. Of the one thousand prisoners from 1971, 895 stayed out of prison. Quite simply, that meant that recidivism fell from 45 percent to 10.5 percent.

Dennie Briggs drew the following conclusion: "We must be ready to abolish a practice when it has been clearly shown not to work."[6]

The experiment that my wife Françoise and I conducted from 1970 to 1978 in our apartment in Porte d'Orléans is just as compelling, though on a much smaller level. At the beginning, Françoise was a pharmacy assistant, then an instructor at the Reflection-Action Prison Justice Association. By the end of the experiment, she no longer worked outside the home. As for me, I was a psycho-socio-therapist at the Therapeutic Center of Rueil-Malmaison and facilitator at the Alésia House, an institution for people leaving prison. Beginning in 1972, I was hired as a psychologist at the psychiatric hospital in Ville-Évrard and lecturer in psychology at Paris VIII University-Vincennes. We took in seventy young people for stays from eight to nine months, with follow-up for each for two to three years after. Several of them were admitted a second time, like Muriel, nicknamed Cuddly BB, and Marco, the teddy boy. They were getting out of prison or the psychiatric ward. Some were not in France legally. A few were dealing with addictions to drugs or to alcohol. Only six went back in, which, by inference, points to a failure rate of 8.5 percent. We took on this hosting in an effort to match our words with action. We were not a foster family. This commitment was completely unpaid and militant.

We had a child, Marc, who was eight years old at the time. He took on an important position with our residents, especially Muriel and Pierrot the junkie, who had a real sibling rivalry with him. This allowed them to make changes, since, while jealous of the "real" son, they also called us Papa Jacques and Mama Françoise. Marc's intelligence and sensitivity often played a key role with certain of the young people. He was funny and would set an example. During a meal, one of the youth, Jeannine said, "I have no idea why I always fall for bad guys." Marc replied coolly, "Maybe you're a masochist." Everyone burst out laughing.

The people formerly incarcerated in prison or the psych ward were between seventeen and thirty-two years old, the eldest having spent twelve years in prison. The core of the experience was sharing life together, in a family atmosphere, and in an anarchist communal context. Our discussions revolved around criminality, illness, drug use, and politics. Two of the most frequent debates were whether it was better to be a criminal or a worker? And should we be politically engaged or only think of ourselves? The issue of mental illness often came up, including borderline and other personality disorders, psychopathy, and schizoidia. Muriel was diagnosed with a personality disorder, Marco the teddy boy as psychopath, Robert and Sylvie were schizophrenic.

Like David Cooper, we had some difficulties with the environment. At Cooper's Villa 21, the neighbors called it a "bunch of lunatics." As for us, they said, "It's a gang of thieves, whores, drug addicts, and Arabs."

On the model of Psychiatria democratica in Italy, and unlike David Cooper, I spoke with all of the shopkeepers on the street. In a world as Manichean as ours, the situation became completely reversed: We had become saints sheltering the needy . . . But we still needed to maintain awareness all the time, because it would only take something small to spark a problem.

One day, Sophie, who was seventeen, and Jean-Luc who was eighteen, had a fight in the dining room and broke the table in half. I was pushed to get angry and made them repair the furniture. They spent hours on it! Another time, a fight broke out between Jean-Luc and a militant from the Marge movement, Walter Jones. I asked them to talk it out outside the apartment . . . Walter ended up with his head in a trashcan on the street!

I explained to them that, in order to avoid putting us in danger, while other people live under our roof, it was strictly forbidden to enter with weapons, hashish and other drugs, and it was forbidden to store stolen goods. And, of course, they couldn't commit any crimes on our street . . . I had to get rid of two guys who had "found" a case of checks . . . I also had to get rid of a P38!

There were two nights when I was woken up by the police: "Are you the guardian of Sophie and Jean-Luc?" Once, they had robbed a gumball machine at the Chelles train station. The second time, they stole all of the interiors of the cars on a road in Vitry . . .

The most serious situation was when I was held in custody at the XIV arrondissement precinct. I didn't know why the police came looking for me. They told me: "We know you are an educator. Sometimes, people mess up by being too close to the youth that they care for." I couldn't believe it. The end of the story came tumbling after, when I saw one of the residents at the time, Guy, show up. He couldn't speak because he had swallowed five Valium in order to have the courage to turn himself in, and thus, to exonerate me!

What happened? Jean-Pierre, another resident, told me the story. My car, an old Aronde P-60, broke down. I had parked it on the ring road. Seeing that I wasn't using it, Guy took it over as a workshop for repainting stolen cars! Jean-Pierre had told Guy: "It could only have been you or me. I know that it's you. If you don't go turn yourself in, I'm going to say it's me. We can't let Jacquot get arrested like that . . ."

One night around 7:30pm, years later, the doorbell rang. I went to open it and found myself face to face with Jean-Pierre! He was talking quickly: "Hi, dear Jacques. I'm here to thank you. I live in Bordeaux. I am a truck driver. I am making a delivery in Paris. I took the opportunity to come see you. Thanks to you, I got out. But I also wanted to say that you're a sucker. The point of life is to make profit and fill your pockets. You have to think of yourself. That's how I live. Anyway, it's because you are the way you are that I was allowed to get where I am today. So, I'm thanking you!"

We gave each other a kiss and he left preening. I realized that he did not end up becoming an anarchist, much less an anti-prison militant, which goes to show that our discussions hadn't been aimed at any indoctrination whatsoever.

Many of these young folks keep me up to date with their lives. Pierrot became a house painter. After prison, psychiatric hospital, the shelter, and an apartment, he discovered a new "heroine," who was a social worker. Marcon sells fruits and vegetables at La Ciotat. Cuddly BB became a receptionist at an International Hostel in Saint-Ouen. Mustapha worked as a special-ed teacher, then assistant director at the Vernon educational center in Eure. Later, he took a position as a street worker for the Emmaüs organization in Villiers-sur-Marne. He finished his career as a director for several of the organization's shelters.

All four of them wanted a book to be published to tell their story and the "House of Lost Cats," as it was called by our primary care doctor, whom we often visited. Each of them wrote a text. I asked specialists to read them and then present their analysis through interviews with me, which would be included in the book. Five of them responded to my request: the Judge Étienne Bloch, of the magistrate union; Father Jaouen, who died in 2015, and who for many years took drug users to detox on his boat, the *Bel Espoir* (Great Hope); Dr. Tomkiewick, head of the abnormal psychology department at Paris VIII-Vincennes and director of Inserm; Serge Adam, a formerly incarcerated person who became the director of the Escale house in Châlons-en-Champagne; and Serge Livrozet, founder of CAP, anti-prison and anarchist militant, who also founded a publishing house in the 1980s, Les Lettres libres (Free Letters).

The Delinquent-Making Machine was published in 1982. In the book, all of the residents spoke about love. In this surrogate family, they found something their parents couldn't give them. Thus they were able to repair themselves, rebuild themselves, and develop a minimal base of narcissism, and therefore discover their own freedom and the respect for others' freedom.

CHAPTER SEVEN

Recent and Current Alternatives
to Incarceration

In the 1980s, a daring lawyer, named Duccio Scatolero, took up the baton. Seriously concerned about the young people incarcerated in the juvenile wing in the Turin prison, he figured out a solution that would make an effective intervention. We met in 1985 in Évry. He believed that one of the best ways to make change was to mobilize the people. He presented a film that had a very clear message. In it, we saw townspeople interviewed about delinquents. Their remarks were distressing, but commonplace: "They are deadbeats. We have to put them in prison. We can't let such dangerous people be free."

Scatolero then had the interviewees visit prison and spoke to them afterwards. Their position was completely transformed: "It's dreadful! That could be our children. They are kept inactive. That's not how they'll be let back out. Prison is not the answer." The lawyer took the opportunity to ask them, "But what else could we do?" The answer came quickly: "We need training workshops so that they learn trades." The following months were devoted to the development of various trainings inside prison: cooking, baking, butchery, mechanics . . . The organization responsible for the trainings had around two thousand members. Many were craftspeople, merchants, and residents from the town. They were highly active and determined to work together to transform the condition of these young incarcerated people.

In the prison at this time, sentences remained rather short. Like in France, the average wasn't more than five months. The trainees were almost all released at the end of their sentence before they'd finished their training. Two options arose: either the craftspeople hired the youth in their own businesses and, thus, they could complete their trainings; or they would end up back inside—which had been the common result—and so those who re-offended could resume their training where they left off and thereby bring it to a successful completion.

The resolution was funny, to say the least. At the end of five years, Scatolero met with the director of the juvenile wing, which had at first incarcerated a hundred people. Now, only eight remained. The director exclaimed to the lawyer: "Mr. Scatolero, you've stolen my prison!"

At the end of the 1980s, a team of teachers from Child and Youth Services established a farm, Laplanche, in a small village, Champoly, between Puy-en-Velay and Saint-Étienne. Juveniles went there instead of going to prison. At first, they renovated the premises as a group, then started growing crops and then raising farm animals. The youth came voluntarily to Champoly. They agreed to undertake agricultural work. By and large, they had been sentenced from six months to two years.

But the activities didn't stop with farm work. The teachers invited groups and organizations from Saint-Étienne to come meet with the residents. They organized cultural trips to the town. The idea behind opening the space was as much for the mobility of the juveniles as for the people coming in from outside. We know that this kind of experiment of "living together" can be quite demanding, even if it is rewarding and especially inspiring. This alternative ended at the beginning of the 2000s. The teachers went back to the Child and Youth Services in Saint-Étienne, but they could be proud of the work they had done, since the outcomes speak for themselves.

Prior to the Laplanche experiment, the people who went into prison had a recidivism rate of 50 percent, a number that matched the national average. Those who participated in the alternative at the farm at Champoly only re-offended at a rate of 22 percent.

The Nivernais Organization of Reintegration Assistance (ANAR) began in 1977 and is still operating. Its longevity is to be admired. ANAR includes forty-four spaces for housing and forty spaces for reintegration jobs. It has several assignments: environment and green space, paper recycling, soft materials, sewing, multipurpose workshop (construction finishing and carpentry).

At the center, four teachers are on duty, with one half-time, and four technical guides are engaged for the reintegration jobs. This organization provides an alternative to prison for its population of delinquents. In some cases, it provides a sentencing reduction. The management reports a very small recidivism rate, which isn't surprising when punishment and incarceration are swapped out for mutual aid and freedom.

There is another area of intervention at ANAR: people responsible for domestic violence. The assignment comes from the Bourges court, and involves a prohibition of going to the home of the person harmed and an assignment to the residence. Furthermore, these people undergo psychological treatment. The outcome proves to be even more compelling than for the other resident group: recidivism is close to zero!

The most important example of a justice system that is alternative to the State is in Guerrero, Mexico. We learned of it thanks to two anarchist militants, Serge and Monique, hosts of the show "Black Holes" on Radio libertaire. They brought me to meet Françoise Neff, an anthropologist who has conducted high-level research in the state of Guerrero. This allowed me to confirm this success story, with the help of the thesis by Yoloth Fuentes Sanchez, graduate of the Latin-American Social Sciences Department in Flasco, Mexico (translated by Bernadette Porcher).

The experiment began in 1992. Attacks, rapes, abductions, cattle theft, and drug trafficking were exploding in the Costa Montaña region. The

Indigenous people of the area lived in fear. The Mexican police did not succeed in arresting the perpetrators, especially since they often collaborated with them. Thirty-six villages of Guerrero came together to create a community police on October 15, 1995. These police came from the Indigenous communities. They quickly found out that if they handed over a delinquent to the State police, they would immediately be released if they had money. And those who were put in prison would go back in immediately after release.

In 1997, the villages decided that the community police should expand their functions to the domain of justice. It was henceforth called the Community Security, Justice, and Reeducation System (SSJRC). The three main principles were: investigate before prosecuting, reconcile rather than judge, and reeducate instead of punish. It was a real cultural revolution when compared to the function of the State. It was even more obvious that it is an extremely advanced way of thinking (compared to ours) that forms the basis of this view of human relations.

Sixty-three villages created the SSJRC. They are made up of Mixtec, Tlapanec, Nalúa, and Mestizo people. This correlated with the six municipalities of Costa Montaña, which has one hundred thousand inhabitants. It is no longer possible to claim that it only works for small populations, like Kakabila or Barbuda. It's not utopian to try to implement this on a bigger scale. But we must also still imagine a great shift in our attitudes. For these Indigenous groups, when an offense or crime is committed, we are all victims: the person who was harmed, of course; but also the person who harmed, because they have lost their speech, that is their honor; and also the collective, because it couldn't keep its member on the right path. When will we be open to this kind of philosophy?

The rest goes without saying. For the SSJRC, prison doesn't exist. Prison doesn't allow re-education and brings no benefit to the villages. People who are arrested undertake community work: building roads, bridges, public buildings ... Re-education occurs through conversations with elders, who instill in them a principle of work and provide them with the training they hadn't received. Whoever harms again has to do a double load of community work. The offenders live, work, and sleep in the villages with the residents. They are not removed from society.

Each village has a police captain, who is nominated through a general assembly every three years. There are 612 community police officers who arrest offenders and ensure security. Of the sixty-three regional captains, six are named to the regional command and make up an executive committee of community police with a one year term.

Over the course of two years, the SSJRC reduced offenses in this region of Guerrero by between 90 and 95 percent. However, the State police continue to harass the SSJRC for "illegal deprivation of freedom." But of course their problem with the SSJRC is something completely different: the community police thwart the scams and tricks of the State police. Mexico cannot support the existence of a parallel system of justice that enforces its own laws and doesn't even use the State prisons!

Let's not be naively optimistic. In the first ten years of SSJRC, five men, police or captains, died while doing their duty. That didn't deter the Indigenous villages, even if it dampened some enthusiasm. For these crimes, an agency was formed from six regional committees that acted as judges: the Regional Coordination of Community Authorities (CRAC). Its goal was to rebuild tradition that also fits a Western model of constitutional founding and respect for international law. The Regional Community Organization (OCR), founded October 15, 1995, confronted the State: "We are not here to ask permission, we are here to inform you of the people's choice."

In the same spirit, in 1996 they decided not to remand any prisoner to the State. The penalty system is based on reparation. Someone steals a chicken worth 50 pesos. If a day of work is worth 25 pesos, the thief owes two days of work to the community. The moral is clear:

> Rather than talk about punishment, we prefer to talk about education and
> re-education, to give a third chance to a human being . . . In the villages

where the person who is condemned goes, they are fed and housed . . . We are moving forward: we are the only region in the state of Guerrero where there are no armed assaults, no hostage-taking. To the government that wants to eliminate the community police and claim it is illegal, we reply that we are the law: "You have power, we don't have money, but we are in the right."

In *Le Rendez-vous de Vicam* [*Visiting Vicam*], Joani Hocquenghem quotes a Tlapanec speaker in the San Luis Acatlán region: "Last night, you saw a film about the community police. I am the captain of my village, and I want to administer justice in my community. We have set an example to people in other countries who visit us, we can address the issues of our communities provided that the people oversee the means of administering justice, that the people have their own framework for security, which is not of the kind that tortures our people."[1]

In her thesis on the SSJRC, Yoloth Fuentes Sánchez explains, "In 1998, in the community of Potrerillo Cuapinole, in the San Luis Acatlán township, the people decided to create a body responsible for explaining and administering community justice (according to the customs and traditions of the villages). That is how the Regional Coordination of Community Authorities (CRAC) in Costa Chica-Montaña de Guerrero was formed."[2] She makes an important point: "Often they don't come to punishment, and simply decide on mediation and reparation of harm . . . The issue is to re-educate, to put the person back on the right path. Prison destroys—we don't. If someone ends up in prison for being violent, prison makes them become more violent and, upon release, even more so."[3] Hence, the conclusion: "The community police system is a legitimate institution for the obtainment and administration of justice. This system has fought for its rights and its continued existence since 1995 and it should be understood as a contribution to democracy, multiculturalism, and legal pluralism."[4]

The idea of open prisons has been around for many years, but it has become more popular recently. Presumably prison administrations on a certain continent have even started to think about it. Obviously, this is not abolition of prison. For those of us who believe that we must not incarcerate human beings on principle, this is not a solution. Prison removes, harms, breaks and even kills. If we are consistent in our thinking, we can't remove an individual from society. The problem should be handled within the collective. Eliminating someone does not remove the conflict—only the individual.

But are so-called modern western civilizations capable of functioning without dungeons, death camps, or deviant disintegration machines? Most are far from it. That is why we must fall back on this idea of open prisons. At this stage of our evolution, we are somewhat forced to have recourse to transitional solutions. Ethically, abolish the prisons. Pragmatically, open the prisons. In Norway, on Bastøy Island, a prison center only holds prisoners and their keepers. It accommodates 150 incarcerated people. Every day, some of them take the ferry to go work in Oslo, the capital, about a hundred kilometers away. Similar experiments exist in Sweden, Finland, Germany (Brelfeld), Switzerland (Witzwil), and even in France (Metz-Queuleu and Casabianda). In the Scandinavian countries, 20 to 30 percent of the carceral population live in open prisons. Further, these countries have closed institutions due to lack of prisoners... We are far behind.

At Bastøy, the salary is the same as in the rest of society. Prisoners owe income tax. They reimburse the victims. They are able to send money to their family without going broke like people held in most European prisons. All of the incarcerated people have access to culture. Schooling is so accessible that there are no illiterate people. The training of supervisors includes two years at university. Of course, the institutions cost much less than traditional prisons. Recidivism has fallen to 16 percent as opposed to 20 percent for the whole of Norway—already much ahead of us. Remember combining all the rates in France, recidivism is 50 percent at minimum. In Sweden, it's 30 percent. In France, without including sentence reductions, recidivism climbs to 63 percent. In the United States, the champions of incarceration, the figure reaches 66 percent. A small island transformed into a detention center, Bastøy is the first ecological and humanist prison in the world. It has no bars and no walls.

The Scandinavian countries are halfway between American Indigenous people and Westerners. In 1945, the penal code in Sweden put it explicitly: "Prisoners are orphans in the Swedish people's house," adding that society must reintegrate them. This is nowhere near the French political hysteria regarding delinquency and criminality. Prison politics are conducted outside of electoral opportunism . . .

The less difficult prison is, the better the odds that reintegration will be easy. Combining the Finnish, Swedish, and Norwegian views seems like repeating the obvious, but these are simply facts. Hannu Kallio, a person incarcerated at the open prison in Kerava in Finland, observes: "You can leave if you want. But if you escape, you will go back to prison. You are better here."

In the 1960s, Scandinavian researchers investigated how effectively punishment lowered crime rates. The result was unequivocal: zero effectiveness. This is what led the current specialist, Tapio Lappi-Seppala, to remark: "It was the first time that such a crucial study took place, which showed that incarceration serves no purpose . . . The Finnish lesson is that it is perfectly possible to decrease recourse to imprisonment by two-thirds, without increasing the crime rate of the country."

The head of the agency for criminal sanctions of this country, Esa Vesterbacka, noted that open prisons cost less: the expense per person is decreased by one-third because needs for staffing and security devices are reduced or eliminated, and residents are lodged in dorms. "That is not the main reason to create this type of prison, but of course, these days, it's not bad to be able to pay less either."

Despite collective reluctance, there is nevertheless another experiment in France that has made a contribution, as it were, to the deconstruction of prison: the Moyembrie farm. It was launched in the Aude region in 1996, when Jacques Pluvinage and his wife welcomed their first resident, a formerly incarcerated person, whom they knew from their visits to prison.

Over the years, more and more people leaving prison came to the farm, and so an organization was created in 2002. They signed an agreement with the minister of justice in 2004. Prisoners in detention (depending on the prison administration) could spend the final twelve months of their sentence there. It was an adjusted sentence.

Two years later, in 2006, Moyembrie was approved as a reintegration workshop site. Residents work twenty hours a week and are paid the minimum wage. In 2009, the farm joined Emmaüs within the framework of its "Solidarity Economy and Integration" program. There they do true agricultural work, gardening, and raise animals, much like Laplanche in Champoly.

Fifty incarcerated people are accommodated each year. In the morning, residents care for the goats, make cheese, work on vegetable gardening, prepare about one hundred baskets of organic products to be sold every week in the region and in Île-de-France. Afternoons are filled with organizing searches (for employment, housing), health appointments, or family visits.

Samuel Gautier, who worked for two years at Moyembrie, along with Nicolas Ferran, OIP lawyer, is seeking funds and support to establish a second farm in the Aude region, at Lespinasse. Their organizational idea is the same as Moyembrie, but the activities will be devoted to ecotourism.

CHAPTER EIGHT

Mediation and Reparation

Moving from the idea of punishment to that of mediation requires a true shift in thinking, bringing us closer to Indigenous culture. And despite what some would like to believe, this is not a regression, but progress. Technological advances do not guarantee any cultural superiority whatsoever; they can even be used to shroud a true social and political darkness.

We are caught up in the idea of guilt. Blame lurks throughout the shadows of our unconscious. The Judeo-Christian tradition hinders our evolution and drags us to the bottom. The pure and harsh Catholicism before Vatican II spread its harmful ideology of sin everywhere. It is not only European countries that are affected. All of the States in the Mediterranean region are subsumed, particularly those in North Africa. Furthermore, the civilizations poisoned by colonialization reproduce the same patterns.

All that remains is the feeling that we should do what is right. Each time we give in to the Sirens of Evil, we are guilty. Thus, we ought to be punished. This venom poisons whole segments of our societies. We assume that since the wrongdoing made the victim suffer, whoever committed the act ought to suffer in order to atone for the harm they caused. The law of retribution is not too far off.

The Abolition of Prison

The kind of progress that gets promoted hypocritically calls this justice. Punishment involves doling out to the convicted person harm that is approximately equal to what the victim suffered. The penal code measures the length and specifics of the punishment depending on the seriousness of the offence. It goes without saying that the suffering of the delinquent doesn't erase that of the person harmed or killed. Some may believe it, but they don't understand that they still operate on the basis of vengeance. Grieving does not inherently work through imposing harm on the guilty person . . .

This prejudice belongs to what we might name an emotional plague. It is connected to hatred, jealousy, desire to destroy—even sadism, and, in certain cases, perversion. Why must we be so twisted?

A true Copernican revolution is necessary. We no longer need this Manichean view that makes us believe there are good people and bad people. It is an obsolete way of thinking. Instead, we must acknowledge that laws exist and the real issue is whether or not we comply with them. When there is an infraction, the law has simply been violated. This might cause harm to a particular member of the social group. We all know that the masses are easily shocked and their emotions are manipulated. We have to be careful. Emotional contagion is rapid, and moves quickly and explodes on a large scale. The reactionary powers know this and shrewdly take advantage of it, which creates a dictatorship of emotions. Whenever a particularly horrible crime is committed, the head of State passes a law, even if ten already exist on the same subject.

It is a bit more rational to say that the punishment is often enough. It involves naming the act: "You have committed this crime." It involved this injury to an individual, or even to the whole of society. From there, what can we do in order to undo the action or repair the consequences that it generated? This does not stop the individual from having feelings about the significance or the seriousness of the violation. We can even assess it according to a scale of values. This would pertain to the field of ethics, which must not be confused with morality or psychology. But let's remain in the domain of reason, even if we continue to be emotional beings. We can be shocked, outraged, or even very angry. That doesn't prevent us from making measured decisions.

What is the best method for settling problems and conflicts within a collective? We all know it: dialogue, reconciliation, discussion—in short, mediation. It has always existed. We could mention the African Palaver Tree and methods of reconciliation. Angela Davis makes this case that, "In limited instances, some governments have attempted to implement alternatives that range from conflict resolution to restorative or reparative justice."[1] In *Burn the Prisons of Apartheid*, Natacha Filippi refers to the Truth and Reconciliation Commission in South Africa: "From now on, every amnesty processes should be preceded by a disclosure of the facts and an encounter between the victims—or the family of victims—and the perpetrators."[2]

The same ideas are expressed in the pamphlet, "Deviancy in Anarchist Society," written by the hosts of the "Ras les murs" radio show: "At any rate, in this context, cooperative work occurs between the victim or that person who represents them and the person who committed the harm."[3] Louk Hulsman reminds us in *Lost Causes* that this has existed for ages: "In the Bantu culture, what matters when someone has killed is not whether they are killed or punished but whether they can repair, usually by working for the family of the victim."[4] He cites an example of mediation from the Netherlands: "The mediator listens to the people separately and prepares a form of compromise that corresponds to what they heard, then suggests a plan to each of the interested parties, and they modify it until it is accepted by everyone."

Among these examples of mediation, or reparation, we can include the timely reminder from Kropotkin: "The principle of the law of retaliation, by which the community gives itself the right to get revenge against the criminal, is no longer acceptable."[5] This way of thinking has existed for a long time. In the article, "A State Without Prisons," in the journal *Esprit*, I wrote: "When guilt is no longer seen as the inherent framework for every felony or criminal act, the concept of punishment will become obsolete."[6] Albert Jacquard states unequivocally: "Once in prison, the guilty person clearly does not engage in reparations for their action."[7]

Now, we all know that after an assault, an act of violence, a rape, or a theft, the person who was attacked wants to understand what happened. Above all, they want to have an explanation for it. This does not escape Jacquard's analysis: "The moral reparation desired by the victim begins in dialogue with the attacker." If you put them in prison, it becomes impossible. Revenge is fulfilled. Mediation does not happen. Albert Jacquard adds: "Not only is the damage caused by the wrongdoing not repaired, but society also sentences itself to bearing the high cost of an incarceration."[8]

Our country lags behind, despite increasing developments elsewhere; however, the French Association for Criminal Mediation, created by Jacqueline Moreno, has existed for a long time. Moreno set a precedent along with Laurène in New Caledonia, who directs the Association of Prison and School Mediation. Some countries, as we see, use this process for many crimes, including murders. Catherine Baker laments, "In France, criminal mediation exists but is only brought into play for petty crimes, mainly for conflicts between neighbors."[9] But this doesn't happen for criminal trials. Thus, once the media has made excessive appeal to public outrage, revenge remains the rule. Catherine Baker shares Albert Jacquard's view: "The idea of a justice that repays evil with evil can only be defended in contempt of all justice."

Let's return to the way the system of community security, justice, and reeducation (SSJRC) in the state of Guerrero works: "Often they don't come to punishment, and simply decide on mediation and reparation of harm."[10] If we speak with such urgency about a necessary shift in our way of thinking, it's because the Indigenous communities of Guerrero show us a path that we have not yet really traveled in order to come to such practices . . . "It is important to consider that the Indigenous regulation amounts to a 'different' way of looking at the world and that it is linked to the reality of their daily life whose centerpiece is the communal life of individuals."[11] The thief can repair the damage that they caused society. In view of such approaches, our system ought to conclude that it is a failure. Thus the need for us to move from a concept of punishment to concepts of dialogue and reconciliation. But a new current of thinking has begun to accumulate over a decade or so, and remains on the periphery. It seems to be powered by exceptional people who lead the way and illuminate our darkness with their visions.

In the 1970s, the singer Julos Beaucarne insisted on meeting the person that had killed his wife. He wanted to explain the harm he had done to her by taking her life and to himself in depriving him of his wife. He then fought so that the killer was not sentenced to death. In 2005, Jean-Paul and Marie-Cécile Chenu wanted to correspond with the three young neo-Nazis who relentlessly kicked their son François in the face because he was gay . . . He had been thrown, still breathing, into a lake. This awful "news story" took place in Reims in September 2002. Only one of them agreed, despite the hesitation of the prison administration, which didn't understand the parents' aim. A truly reparative relationship was then built between the parents and this young man.

The consensus of all of these insights points towards the abolition of prison. Only the lack of imagination perpetuates incarceration as the solution to crimes and misdemeanors. The prison walls are simply the petrification of these ideas.

Numerous alternatives exist in terms of the law itself: judicial review; community service; suspended sentences; probation; ankle monitors; carrying out the sentence on weekends; warnings; *Habeas Corpus* in the French understanding; fines; suspension of license for driving, fishing, hunting; house arrest; work detail; and day parole are all types of alternative sentences. We can't claim that nothing has been proposed outside of prison. The main problem lies in the fact that these alternatives haven't stopped rampant overcrowding of prisons. Furthermore, without exception, this arsenal remains in the spirit of penalty, that is suffering, and hence punishment. A system that doesn't want to change and that conforms with the international economic model remains deeply unjust. We have known for a long time that a large number of crimes and offenses are committed as a result of social inequality, i.e., poverty or even destitution.

Let's suppose, according to liberal logic, that it is a lesser evil. Humanists of this school of thought have understood that the pain inflicted is neither therapeutic nor a deterrent. It simply ruins people and does not take part in the lawmaker's desire to set an example; at the very least, it does not eliminate delinquency or criminality at all.

It would be better if these steps were seriously taken towards the shift in mindset our society needs so badly. When judges start to turn consistently to alternatives in order to avoid prison, breaking with the concepts of guilt and punishment, a great step will have been taken. We are far away from that, even if some of the population is becoming aware.

To return to mediation... perhaps it's difficult for Europeans to acknowledge that a return to the roots of American Indigenous people, Australian Aboriginal people, and the peoples of equatorial and South Africa, is a prerequisite to achieving more justice and humanity. In particular, we need to be inspired by the residents of Guerrero and of Chiapas, who practically operate through direct democracy. In any case, we are aware that a great number of Indigenous communities are organized along anarchist lines.

In *La Justice réparatrice* [*Restorative Justice*], Stéphane Jacquot writes, "The goal of justice is to restore the balance that was broken between the society and the person who committed the crime or offence by finding a connection between the trial that would punish and the effect of reparation on the victim, the person who harmed, and society."[12] This describes exactly where we are today. Justice occurs in addition to a trial and not instead. Progress will have been made only once it fits the definition Stéphane Jacquot gives further on: "Overall, restorative justice is geared towards three goals: reparation for the victim, accountability for the person who harmed, and restoring social peace."[13]

The criminologist Robert Cario and the judge Denis Salas, who oversaw the publication of *Oeuvres de justice et victims* [*Works of Justice and Victims*], volume one, provide their explanation: "This type of recognition between the people involved in the offence restores self-esteem with understanding and acceptance of the harm caused by the offence."[14] Like other authors, they insist on the fact that mediation produces reparation involving the person who harmed, the victim, and the community: "Restorative practices don't exclusively aim at the damaged relationships between the implicated people, they also affect the social relations that have been disrupted by the harm."

In volume two of *Works of Justice and Victims: Victims, From Trauma to Restoration* (*Oeuvres de justice et victims. Victimes: du traumatisme à la restauration*), Robert Cario prefers the term "restorative justice," which involves the person who harmed, the victim, and society, while, in his view, "mediation" refers instead to the meeting between offender and victim. He adds a very important point: "Restorative justice aims for a result where the victims, offenders, and the community have the 'sense of satisfaction' that 'justice was done.'"[15] The ideas of public opinion and the majority are more theoretical and political abstractions than reality. They come from so many different factors that it is absurd to try to pin them down and generalize them. Robert Cario attests: "Each time, we find that a majority of respondents prefer a reaction aimed towards reparations instead of a punitive reaction."[16] That might seem surprising, but it turns out that in such situations the desire for revenge and punishment completely vanishes. This is exactly what the criminologist reports again in another book, *Les rencontres détenus-victimes. L'humanité retrouvée* [*Meetings Between Incarcerated People and Victims: Humanity Rediscovered*]: "Being socialized in this way, the desire for 'revenge' disappears to make room for mutual understanding."[17] This book very accurately reports on the experience of meetings between incarcerated people and victims at the central prison in Poissy in 2010.

What becomes clear is that the prisoners were able to let go of the image they had of the hateful and vengeful victim. Similarly, the victims gave up the stereotype of the unemotional and violent monster. One prisoner said at the end of the process, "I saw firsthand the harm caused to the victims."[18] The victims arrive at a kind of reciprocity of feeling. One of them describes it in this way: "Their increasingly deeper awareness of the mess caused by the criminal act and its irreversibility seemed to reinforce the desire to rebuild themselves, which they have already begun to do, and that demands our admiration."[19] Robert Cario concludes beautifully: "The deconstruction of the figure of the 'monster' and that of the 'vengeful victim' does its job."[20]

Our evolution is slow. This progress is still very recent, and it must be continued and expanded. Stéphane Jacquot confirms, "In the 1980s, criminal mediation started in prosecutors offices, and then was formalized by a law on January 4 1993. Criminal mediation is an alternative measure that allows 'petty offenders' to plead guilty and to repair the harm from their actions directly to the victims."[21]

Maryse Vaillant, a psychologist at the Youth Legal Protection, closely followed this development and reported on it in her wonderful book, *La Réparation* [*Reparation*]: "For the minor delinquent, adolescent in crisis, or runaway youth, the act of reparation—while not forgetting the law—makes them understand the consequences that their actions can have in other people's lives."[22] It also performs other invaluable benefits: "The main idea behind the approach of reparation lies in the belief that each person can answer for the actions that they commit and the harms that they cause without having to pay the price of their freedom or of their dignity."[23] She adds an essential point: "Reparation repairs self-esteem."[24] Maryse Vaillant and Robert Cario agree in thinking that mediation, reparation, and restorative justice ought gradually to replace repression, and thus prison. Vaillant puts it in this way: "As long as reparation is only used in a very limited and partial way, the process cannot demonstrate its true educational benefit, and thus cannot persuade or propose a feasible alternative to the old repressive solutions."[25] Cario makes greater haste: "In the long run, restorative justice should not play along with criminal justice. It should fight against it."[26]

Instead of prison, mediation.

CHAPTER NINE

How Do We Get Abolition?

A question of principle comes up: are we talking about prevention or of revolution? We will leave the responsibility of answering this question to the individual. In any case, Peter Kropotkin puts it clearly: "Let us assure to every child a sound education and instruction, both in manual labor and science, so as to permit him to acquire, during the first twenty years of his life, the knowledge and habits of earnest work—and we shall be in no more need of dungeons and jails, of judges and hangmen."[1]

We know that we are not yet there. Our society operates in such a way that countless young people fall through the cracks, so we should not be surprised that there is madness, delinquency, and terrorism. Every time something happens, people complain: "We didn't see this coming." But the liberal system only foresees profit. Of course, it would be desirable to consider prevention, in the spirit of what Wilhelm Reich called "children of the future."

Angela Davis returns to Victor Hugo's thought: "School can therefore be seen as the most powerful alternative to jails and prisons."[2] The issue of the abolition of prison is so distressing to some that it always provokes the same reaction: "But what would you replace it with?" This is not actually the problem. We must transform social logic. Replacing what we eliminate with an equivalent would mean absolutely nothing. Without going to the point of revolution, which would be a radical solution, there still remain a number of means. Let's not hide them. Angela Davis compiles a list: "In other words, we would not be looking for prison-like substitutes for the prison, such as house arrest safeguarded by electronic surveillance bracelets. Rather, positing decarceration as our overarching strategy, we would try to envision a continuum of alternatives to imprisonment—demilitarization of schools, revitalization of education at all levels, a health system that provides free physical and mental care to all, and a justice system based on reparation and reconciliation rather than retribution and vengeance."[3] She adds, this "can also include job and living wage programs, alternatives to the disestablished welfare program, community-based recreation, and many more."[4]

Furthermore, in the spirit of Louk Hulsman, Albert Jacquard raises a question already considered by those who work in mediation and reparation: "Why not invite the concerned parties in a neighborhood to meet to find a way to repair a damage that has been committed?"[5] This is interesting because it deals with community-based reconciliation. A community would not set in motion an enormous justice machine that ends up being inhuman and anonymous.

The genetic scientist makes plenty of other suggestions. One already exists, but it is only rarely used: "Requiring offenders to play a useful role during a certain amount of time in a hospital where accident victims are cared for and patiently rehabilitated; witnessing the struggle of a person who is trying to rediscover the use of their body, supporting their family, helping each endure the difficulty of hospitalization; so many daily reminders of the consequences of acts similar to what the guilty person has committed."[6]

In the case concerning contaminated blood, Dr. Garretta was sentenced to prison time. It would have been much more appropriate to require him to work for an equivalent amount of time with people living with AIDS . . .

We don't lack examples. In *In Place of Prison*, Dennie Briggs refers to the British doctor, Larry Dye, a former criminal, who in 1974 hosted three young former delinquents in his home. And he mentions the organization KRUM in Sweden, which was established in 1966 with powerful momentum: "Ex-prisoners and intellectuals called a 'Thieves' Parliament' to set forth their case. They fought to give prisoners more rights and influence; to abolish prisons."[7]

Which goes to show that everything is connected. In Sweden, as in France, these struggles are closely linked. They move in the same direction. This brings us back to GIP, CAP, and ASPF. Dennie Briggs sums it up in a phrase: "All of us, if we are to grow and change, need models to live by, not leaders."[8]

Alternatives have existed for a long time. One that is absolutely central has been in the United States since 1973: "'Diversion' is the term which refers to halting or suspending formal action of criminal proceedings against a person on the condition, assumption, and agreement that he will do something in return."[9] The psychologist concludes: "Diversion from the criminal justice system is based on the belief that active help before the trial can change a defendant's life and enable him to become more socially productive."[10]

In *Lost Causes: Must We Get Rid of Prisons?*, Dominique Vernier collects answers to the question, how do we achieve abolition? She begins, "First off, empty the prisons of those who don't belong there: people who are elderly or sick, minors, drug users, people living with AIDS, people with mental illness."[11] One idea always comes up regarding minors: "But here too we still have to invent other structures, which would preferably be schools rather than prisons. Places where young people would have a chance to rebuild themselves, to take shape, and not to be destroyed and overcome by loathing for themselves and others."[12] Regarding drug users, the journalist believes that they are ill people to be helped rather than criminals to lock up. She addresses the cause instead of the effects: "But we must above all implement decriminalization in advance of drug use, just as Portugal and Belgium have done."[13] Concerning people without documents, she has a partially correct opinion: "The goal would be to decriminalize unlawful residence or only to impose a fine."[14]

To give an economic punishment to people who, for the most part, are completely impoverished is, at the very least, absurd. It would be more consistent to abolish borders. We belong less and less to countries, and more and more to continents. What are we waiting on in order to finally be consistent?

Dominique Vernier refers to a wonderful experiment in Austria: "The prosecutor in Linz sentences forty-five young neo-Nazis, arrested during the dismantling of a vast network in 1999, to take courses for a year at the University of Linz in history and democracy (without doing so they would have received a prison sentence for belonging to these organizations)."[15] She highlights the fact that in the Netherlands there is a system of *numerus clausus* that does not allow prison overcrowding to exceed 103 percent. In France, this number is instead 125 percent. Remember, Dominique Vernier's book was published in 2002. She makes the following conclusion: "In the end, calculating for the most part according to official numbers from the Ministry of Justice, it seems possible to release between 14,000 to 22,000 people from French prisons, depending on the different scenarios mentioned."[16] Even if culturally we are so far from the Indigenous people in Guerrero, such that we don't even seem to belong to the same planet, scholars of community policing implement policies that we are beginning to make our own: "In particular, within the security and community justice system, they try to understand the offender so that they can help them gain awareness during rehabilitation of the reasons for the offense and the error that they committed so they may undertake reparation."[17]

Fitting the focus of his book, Arnaud Gaillard brings our attention in *Sexuality and Prison* to the disturbing circumstances that the ostrich of democracy does not wish to see: "If freedom means putting an end to a situation of temporary confinement, how does this perspective make any sense when there are no current guidelines; self-esteem is debased; and deprivation and violence, built up over time during long sentences, results in a hatred of the institution and the society that authorizes it?"[18]

The only sense we can make of it is that prison is a machine that manufactures criminals. When sadness and despair have been overcome, the only thing remaining is hatred and anger. Human beings have their limits. They need hope in order to live. If breathing room is cut off, the instinct for life becomes diseased. It turns towards violence, the desire for revenge, sadism, or even masochism. It is an emotional plague, as we have already observed. The explanation shouldn't be surprising: "The analysis of the experience of sexuality in detention highlights the concept of social death, understood as a death of another kind, at odds with what reintegration might mean."[19]

It's up to us professionals, militants, former prisoners, to see what we must do in order to reverse the process! We can't continue to act as if we didn't know. In the magazine *Esprit* in 1972, Jean-Marie Domenach, a member of GIP, wrote: "We must create institutions and behaviors that treat the causes of offenses rather than responding with repression, and thus require us to transform a society that more and more creates the conditions for criminality."[20]

Let's go back to the paths opened by Robert Cario and Denis Salas: "In many countries, there are programs of mediation and reconciliation between the victim and the offender built upon an understanding of the specific needs of the victims stemming from practical research into a more meaningful and effective approach to delinquency."[21] But their view is uncompromising. They make this diagnosis: "The impact of mediation programs remains rather marginal in the global context of criminal justice administration."[22]

More practically, Jacques Colombat gives an example that can be reproduced: "In Denmark, 60% of incarcerated people are in open prisons; there are some escapes, but in 2008, there were no suicides, while there were five in the closed prisons."[23] This only reinforces the validity of the author's suggestion: "We must stop regarding surveillance cameras, intercoms, one-way internal televisions, tags and beepers as progress. These only replace supervisors, further isolating incarcerated people, which produces distrust, aggression, and violence."[24] The lessons of history are not learned. However, there is no lack of examples: "Primitive societies unaware of State laws operated on other foundations without relying on carceral punishment. Their solutions could still be cruel, but above all they sought reparation, reconciliation, before coming in the last instance to the exile of the offender."[25]

We can't resist reporting one unique experience mentioned by Jacques Colombat:

> Alexander Maconochie, a British Royal Marine officer in the beginning of the 19th century, created a point system. Rather than sentence someone to a time of incarceration, he commuted the sentence into an amount of work to accomplish, measured according to a number of points. Prisoners could reduce the time of their sentence by participating in common tasks. In 1840, the British government named him as the head of the prison on Norfolk Island, a remote island between New Zealand and New Caledonia. On arriving, the island held 1,400 incarcerated people described as "the worst of the worse men." The results of this system were that out of 920 incarcerated people liberated between 1840 and 1844, only 20 went back inside.[26]

Fortunately, openings are beginning to emerge. But they come so slowly! "In May 2010, the fact-finding study of the Ministry of Justice observed: risks arising from prisons without bars would be offset by the benefits for society and incarcerated people with regard to reintegration and humanization of prisons; in the view of society, it might become an acceptable risk."[27]

Just as prescient as Kropotkin, James Guillaume published *Ideas on Social Organization* in 1876. At a time where our technology did not yet exist, he envisioned a system close to that of Guerrero: "This service, which can be called (if the phrase has not too bad a connotation) the Communal Police, will not be entrusted, as it is today, to a special, official body; all able-bodied inhabitants will be called upon to take turns in the security measures instituted by the commune."[28] He organizes violations into two classes: "Cases that fall in the first category, crimes, will henceforth be the responsibility of the security service, who will seek to prevent them, and the responsibility of medical service, who will decide what approaches to take regarding criminals. As for cases in the second category, disputes between people, organizations, communities, they will be judged by arbiters chosen by the parties, as is already done today in many situations."[29]

The abolition of prison is possible.

CHAPTER TEN

Why Abolition?

When starting the radio show "Ras les murs," on Radio Libertaire (89.4) in February 1989, we wanted to take as our standard an excerpt from Kropotkin's *Words of a Rebel:*

> Burn the guillotines, demolish the prisons, drive away the judge, the policeman, the spy—an impure race if ever there was one—but treat as a brother him who has been led by passion to do ill to his kind; above all deprive the truly great criminals, those ignoble products of bourgeois idleness, of the possibility of parading their vices in seductive form, and you can be sure that we shall no longer have more than a very small number of crimes to point to in our society. Apart from idleness, what sustains crime is law and authority; the laws on property, the laws on government, the laws with their penalties and punishments. And Authority, which takes on itself to make these laws and apply them.[1]

Over the soundtrack of *A Clockwork Orange,* this excerpt allowed us to point to the two priorities of the anti-prison struggle: improving conditions of incarceration and abolishing prison.

The Abolition of Prison

At the end of *Lost Causes*, Dominique Vernier asks the fateful question: "What risks is society ready to take so that human beings in violation of the law at some point are able to resume their place in society?"[2]

Angela Davis's answer may surprise some: "A more productive version of feminism would also question the organization of state punishment for men as well and, in my opinion, would seriously consider the proposition that institution as a whole—gendered as it is—calls for the kind of critique that might lead us to consider its abolition."[3] The militant anti-prison movement has developed a very important argument in the United States, which could absolutely be implemented in France and Europe: "If we are willing to take seriously the consequences of a racist and class-biased justice system, we will reach the conclusion that enormous numbers of people are in prison simply because they are, for example, black, Chicano, Vietnamese, Native American or poor, regardless of their ethnic background."[4]

Particularly in France, we can especially refer to the situation of Arabs and Black people, even if other ethnicities have begun to join them in prison. But the reason is quite simple: people with a foreign background have difficulty integrating into the middle and upper classes of society. They automatically fill the ranks of the sub-proletarian, in other words, the poor and marginalized. Angela Davis highlights an issue that I faced at the Bois-d'Arcy jail: "Despite the important gains of antiracist social movements over the last half century, racism hides from view within institutional structures, and its most reliable refuge is the prison system."[5]

It's true, but we must also include psychiatric hospitals and all the institutions that concentrate power at the top of a hierarchy. That helps create the unavoidable conditions for totalitarian violence. Kropotkin had no illusions. With *In Russian and French Prisons*, he gave us a helpful reminder: "People are people; and you cannot give so immense an authority to people over people without corrupting those to whom you give the authority. They will abuse it; and their abuses of it will be the more unscrupulous, and the more felt by the abused, the more limited and narrow is the world they live in."[6]

We only need to recall the abuses of trans prisoners by overseers a few years ago at Fleury-Mérogis. They offered them pounds of sugar and packages of butter in exchange for sexual favors. The feminist Angela Davis does not overlook this: "We found that male correctional employees have vaginally, anally, and orally raped female prisoners and sexually assaulted and abused them."[7] She extrapolates this information to a global scale: "Studies on female prisons throughout the world indicate that sexual abuse is an abiding, though unacknowledged, form of punishment to which women, who have the misfortune of being sent to prison, are subjected."[8]

We can only agree with the American militant that this radical argument goes in the direction of abolition. A trivial but very wise comment by Dominique Vernier makes us think that nothing is impossible: "Some institutions that seem eternal have ended up becoming obsolete or getting abolished."[9]

The arguments that have been proposed are so numerous that arguments for revenge and security often seem more symptomatic of hatred and fear. The architects Augustin Rosenstiehl and Pierre Sartoux propose an argument that too few have made: "Debasement, infantilization, deprivation of intimate relations with family, prolonged isolation, and white torture are not part of the law, which officially condemns these practices. We think that these tendencies are the principle factors that currently make prison a place that creates criminals, since they foster hatred (of society) and frustration (by feeling excluded)."[10]

Many others have reported on the hatred, anger, and rebellion that stem not only from confinement but also the conditions of incarceration. Never being able to open a door, not having any responsibilities, always depending on the whim of a guard, waiting to the point of no longer knowing what you are waiting for, wasting away in emotional and sexual solitude without much hope for tomorrow—this amounts to dying a slow death.

Kropotkin tell us something we can easily discover: "[the prisoner] learns to hate the section of society to which their humiliation belongs, and proves their hatred by new offenses against it."[11] Albert Jacquard draws out the main implication of this experience: "Prison is a place of non-respect."[12] It's not difficult to draw this lesson from the circumstances: "the person who is shut up in a prison is so far from being bettered by the change, that they come out more resolutely the foe of society than they were when they went in."[13]

With tongue-in-cheek, we might say that is the outcome in the best of cases. The prisoner didn't commit suicide, didn't go mad, and didn't escape! We know that some people fall apart bit by bit until they become absolute social wrecks. We see many like this in the homes for the recently released. Without forgetting as well those who, after an overly long incarceration, are afraid of a world that seems hostile to them. The day of their release, they come back to knock on the prison door: "Take me back. I can't do it. It's too hard."

Kropotkin encountered these abandoned people: "a life which a person can endure for years, but which they cannot endure if they have no aim beyond this life itself without being depressed and reduced to the state of a machine which obeys, but has no will of its own; a life which results in an atrophy of the best qualities of the human and a development of the worst of them, and, if much prolonged, renders the person quite unfit to live afterwards in a society of free fellow-creatures."[14]

It is conventional to believe that, as long as they are incarcerated, criminals can no longer harm the collective. This reassures a large portion of the public. We will restate that this is only short-term safety. In this regard, we share Albert Jacquard's perspective. With a recidivism rate worse than that of primary offenses—that is, when the person commits an offense for the first time—we ought to admit that prison doesn't fulfill its mission of reintegration. It promotes recidivism, which contributes to the hardening of the incarcerated person, making their actions worse.

Catherine Baker makes an indisputable sociological analysis: "Prison poses a threat to us: it creates all of the conditions of an ongoing disaster because it casts out people who've been made to suffer intolerable violence in order to punish them. The punishment brings with it so much hatred that allowing it to take place in our name can only destroy us."[15]

Just as with the death penalty, prison has never deterred delinquents and criminals. People who commit offenses think more or less explicitly that they won't get caught. This is particularly true for those who, at the end of their rope, decide to do one "last job!" Louk Hulsman supports this: "Everyone can recognize that the actual existence of the prison system in no way prevents homicides, armed robbery, or break-ins."[16] This observation, however, agrees with the views of all of the specialists of the prison world: "In the end, criminal justice and prison only end up increasing the number of anti-social people and repeat offenders."[17] A lawyer ahead of his time, he takes this logic to a point no one would have expected: "The law defines crime, thus the law creates the criminal!"[18] And it does this on a massive scale!

We have been talking for a long time about overcrowding. Today, there are more than 78,000 incarcerated people. From his personal knowledge, Albert Jacquard reminds us what people tend to forget given the extent of their fear: "Protecting society from individuals who could be labeled as clearly dangerous only means dealing with fewer than 3,000 or 4,000 cases."[19] This covers rape, murder, hostage situations, assault with a deadly weapon, shootings and mass murder—that is, 5 percent of the total of those who are convicted. The rest is made up of people incarcerated for minor offenses which are the overwhelming majority of crimes. We don't need to try too hard to end up with a political analysis. Louk Hulsman puts it quite well: "Obviously the prison system creates and reinforces social inequality." Hence Catherine Baker's logical response: "The struggle against delinquency necessarily begins with a tooth and nail political struggle against poverty."[20]

Just like Loïc Wacquant, Angela Davis emphasizes the economic issue. The evolution of prisons into private, multinational corporations highlights the fact that the carceral system is increasingly about profit. One of its main aims is profitability: "In the meantime, corporations associated with the punishment industry reap profits from the system that manages prisoners and acquire a clear stake in the continued growth of prison populations."[21] This requires the historical focus that Angela Davis shows so well: "The process through which imprisonment developed into the primary mode of state-inflicted punishment was very much related to the rise of capitalism and to the appearance of a new set of ideological conditions."[22]

When fear dictates the rules of political life, we inevitably fall into despotism, the reign of populism and demagoguery. And the laws follow, weaving an inescapable web for the marginalized, non-citizens, people with mental illness, and delinquents. Fortunately, it is possible for us to change governance and to achieve more social justice. Dennie Briggs holds this view: "the argument of this book is that we must be ready to abolish a practice when it has been clearly shown not to work." He also makes this statement of principle, as we have already noted: "We have reached the point when decisive action needs to be taken on a large scale. Such action can succeed."[23]

In 1972, Jean-Marie Deomnach wrote: "It is indeed a matter of tearing down the prison walls, of destroying the prison world, which does not mean, as people pretend to believe, jumping overnight into a world without sanctions."[24] Quite the contrary, it makes us return in a deeper way to concepts that we have already elaborated. If we want to make progress in terms of justice and prison, we will need to give up the idea of guilt. This idea impairs our thinking and sinks us into the miasmas of the past. This idea of guilt, which develops directly from our monotheistic religions, makes us lose our minds. It clouds our thinking.

The idea of guilt is passed down from generation to generation, from civilization to civilization. When we do not follow a rule, we are guilty. We should feel shame. Since suffering is so widespread, the act ought to be measured on the basis of the suffering it has caused. And as we've seen, for a punishment, the person who harms should suffer as much as the person that they made their victim. This come directly from the law of vengeance. We no longer say: "An eye for an eye, a tooth for a tooth." But we strive to make justice really justice.

I urge us to be more reasonable. Let us allow emotions into our hearts, but we can't permit them to direct our thought. It is possible and even desirable to move towards a stage where we think that, as long as there are laws, a violation should be treated in a generous and rational way. Tony Peters writes in *Work of Justice and Victims,* volume 1: "Beyond repression, retribution, and rehabilitation, the idea of a right to reparation works as a third way to achieve practical and direct solutions."[25]

If we give up the idea of guilt, we can return to the idea of offence. Once again, the sanction consists in identifying guilt. It is a symbolic act that replaces punishment. The will to punish, thus to make suffer, gives way to the will to deliver justice. We know the way to do this; we have extensively discussed it above. It is handled through reconciliation, mediation, and leads to an agreement that takes shape through reparation, when the two parties have been able to hear each other. We know that it is being done more and more ... Recall the Indigenous people in the sixty-three villages of Guerrero, which today number almost eighty. They manage their conflicts without recourse to the prisons of the State of Mexico.

Clearly, they don't need our theoretical writing about justice and prison to discover solutions that lead to social peace. They have their own wisdom regarding the cosmos, the earth, and life in society that allows them to harmonize the individual with the collective. They do it basically through self-management, without having read Bakunin or Kropotkin.

In *Are Prisons Obsolete?,* Angela Davis proposes a clear methodology. It is also a warning: "The first step, then, would be to let go of the desire to discover one single alternative system of punishment that would occupy the same footprint as the prison system."[26] The aim of the alternative is to end repression. Let's leave our fears for a moment and share a laugh with Alain Brossat: "If you live in a way that you don't have much to fear from the thief, then you will feel relieved of a big part of your obsession with security."[27]

To expand the analysis, let's spend a moment on the issue of sex offenders, who are used as the supreme argument for keeping spaces of imprisonment. At the end of the twentieth century and beginning of the twenty-first, Dr. Roland Broca, then chief of staff in a public health institution in the Paris region, formed an ethics committee on the treatment of sex offenders.

He brought together a few dozen psychiatrists, psychologists, psychotherapists, psychoanalysts, and experts in this problem, in order to find solutions. We came to propose an alternative place, still in the Paris area, where these prisoners could be treated.

They would be taken from the penitentiary institutions where they did not belong. There, they are called *pointeurs*, and bullied by the other incarcerated people. The center wouldn't be a prison, but instead a secure point of care. Psychotherapy and psychoanalysis would not be mandatory. The caregivers would attempt to incentivize meetings with eventual patients. If that resulted in real work, it would take place as two part therapy: psychiatry for drug therapy, and psychology or psychoanalysis for psychotherapy. Experts would come each year to meet with the clients and decide if they could leave the center, on furlough or for good. These experts would be neutral, since none of them would have taken part in the therapies.

This committee made valuable insights, but it didn't succeed in opening the planned institution. To do so today, it would only be a matter of returning to the idea with new participants, while also calling on some of those who had been part of the committee.

Another committee, named Justice and Chaplaincy of Prisons (*Justice et aumônerie des prisons*), met at Versailles on March 22, 1978. The pastor Maurice Hammel, from the Protestant Federation of France, reported: "To conclude, it seems that these brief remarks about the regime of high security, a specific and tragic development of the general regime of incarceration, clearly highlight the need for careful consideration of measures to be taken to achieve the abolition of prison."[28]

More recently, Gabi Mouesca offered this thought: "The idea of keeping human beings locked up in concrete and barbed wire is unacceptable to me ... I dream of putting all the screws out of work and putting an end to prison." He adds: "To be an abolitionist means fighting against all prisons. The strongest prisons are those of our beliefs, our prejudices, our daily cowardice. Abolitionism has existed as long as prison has existed. In my view, this political movement is a movement of the future; it represents the victory of life over death, the victory of civilization over barbarism. For prison is only barbarism."[29]

It would thus be to our advantage to put an end to this archaic and truly obsolete institution, to use Angela Davis's term. We were able to end the death penalty because it is completely inhuman. It is impossible to defend life while putting anyone to death. Similarly, it is foolish to defend freedom while locking up a living being. If we hope to protect property with prison, it is time to ask ourselves to what extent we can accept that there is such inequality in our society.

Thierry Lodé is professor of animal biology at the Universities of Angers and Rennes, as well as the director of research at the latter. He writes in *Ban public*: "But I claim that yes, it is possible to abolish this dishonorable prison system, it is even, quite simply, necessary to do it in order to leave behind the old world of dead end medieval vengeance where prison still wallows. Yes, progress is nothing but the realizing of utopias, as Oscar Wilde said."[30]

The *Envolée* team, in *Backs Against the Wall*, takes up this perspective, also defended by Henri Lefebvre who called himself a utopian: "A world without prisons is the least that we can dream of."[31] But the collective warns us: "We will not have achieved transformation if the abolition of prisons turns into imprisonment without walls."[32] So many people have insisted on this. Particularly, a ruthless book by Ira Levin describes a completely plausible future world in *This Perfect Day*. Even those who challenge and escape are caught by the leaders. Happiness is mandatory, orchestrated, structured and regulated by a totalitarian system that is no longer possible to destroy.

We are not the owners of even the smallest part of this earth. This planet instead shelters us. What is our power then, if it isn't the illusion of ruling over a planet that doesn't follow our orders, but just rotates around the sun?

The abolition of prison is an act of safety, of solidarity, of mutual aid, and community. But it is also the victory of justice, of ethics, and of freedom.

Appendix

Prison should cease to exist. At the beginning of the twenty-first century, it persists as a relic of other times and other morals. It continues its march of misery and hate. A space of non-life and no rights, this archaic cruelty remains a space of systematic destruction of the individual. We must transform minds, to reach the deep causes that keep it going, since the proof of its failure has already been shown. Anarchists want to break the criminal silence that surrounds the struggle of prisoners and report on the carceral and legal realities. We include this fight as part of the larger struggle for a society without class or State. It will be victorious when the right of the strongest and the law of powerful has vanished.

Prison has done its time, let it die!

Ras les murs

Interview with Jacques and
Nicole Lesage de La Haye

The interview reprinted here was conducted by Nicolas Norrito and Géraldine Doulut and was published in the twelfth issue of *Barricata*, an antifascist and anarchist zine, in June 2004.

How long has the radio show "Ras les murs" existed?

Jacques: Since 1989. On Radio libertaire (RL), there has been a show about prison since the founding of the station in 1981. The first team included Floréal. In 1988, another show began, replaced in 1989 with "Ras les murs." It was made up of former members of the Prisoner Action Committee (CAP), particularly Nicole and me, who had been contacted to start a new version of the show. We asked Bernard to join us as engineer, as he was already working at RL.

Nicole: Following a decision made by the Anarchist Federation's (FA) congress, the hosts of the show were supposed to belong to the FA. We were anarchists, but not with the FA. We joined the historic group

Camillo-Berneri, since Pascal from "*Ras les murs*" was also a member, as well as Serge Livrozet, another founder of CAP in the 1970s.

You have already mentioned CAP a few times in a short amount of time. Could we learn more about this Committee?

Jacques: Before CAP, we must point out that there was Prison Information Group (GIP), started in 1971 with Michel Foucault, Pierre Vidal-Naquet, Daniel Defert, some formerly incarcerated people, and myself. That lasted a year. We put out a few pamphlets, including "The Intolerable Ones: List of the Demands of the Rebellions of 1971" ("Les Intolérables. Cahier des revendications des mutineries de l'année 1971"), a handbook for arrest, and three or four more that followed—but that was the first. Serge Livrozet joined us. He had been released at that time from the central prison of Melun (now a detention center). Serge thought that intellectuals should not be speaking for prisoners, only the prisoners had the right to speak of prison. People like Foucault were uncomfortable, but they came around. In the meantime, they created the Association for the Defense of Prisoner's Rights (ADDD—Association pour la défense des droits des détenus). I started working with CAP with the idea that prisoners would take charge of the struggle, even though I wasn't completely against intellectuals. Remember that there were many individual movements at the time (the disabled, MLF, French Migrant Committee (Comités français immigrés), Asylum Information Group (Group informations asiles), etc.).

Nicole: It's worth noting that virtually all of these movements followed anarchist tendencies.

When were you in prison?

Jacques: I went down in 1957, I was released in 1968. I then tried to survive doing totally shitty jobs, docker, mover . . . In 1957, I was eighteen. I was released at thirty and that is when I started my life as a militant in earnest. My only political awakening in prison was the idea of forming a prisoner union, an idea that only saw light in 1985 with the Prisoner Union Organization (Association syndicale des prisonniers), formed by the prisoners themselves. It was made up of seventeen hundred of the forty-two thousand prisoners at the time. The president was Jacques Gambier, in Fleury-Mérogis. They asked me to be the external president. They had nothing in prison before 1974, no television, no newspapers, nothing...

Nicole: Anyway, Jacques was a little thug...

Jacques: Yes, I was a thief. It was the repression that led to my awakening. I was already anarchist, I became anarchist around seventeen, but I thought that anarchism was the Bonnot Gang. I tried to join the communists, I even went as far as traveling to Romania. As I was being chased with machine guns, I thought that I couldn't belong to this group... My awakening goes back to 1971–1972, with the GIP. Next, all the actions of the CAP were openly anarchist and truly aggressive. For me, this is still the best example of the anti-prison struggle, and I know that everything that I've seen or done since is only a second-rate substitute. I'm not nostalgic, I am simply a bit hopeless politically seeing the shit we have to deal with today when we demand the abolition of prison. I have the same positions as when I was in the CAP, where we fought for abolition, along with militants who also were fighting like crazy inside the prisons—it was amazing.

Can you talk about the struggles of prisoners during the 1970s?

Jacques: There were lots of rebellions in 1974, they were everywhere. We have to note that the Maoists had just been arrested, Livrozet was basically Maoist, but he later swung towards the anarchist tendency. When you look at all of the people from the March 23 movement, few were anarchist ...

The March 23 movement?

The Abolition of Prison

Jacques: March 23, 1968! Yes, we had another March 23, in 1979, at the Opera. That was the end of my dream. That day, I figured out that we were not longer making a revolution. Up till then, I believed. On March 23, 1979, we had four hundred thousand people demonstrating, there were the steelworkers from Longwy, and us, the autonomists; all hell broke loose, there was looting of one part of Paris, but it wasn't the revolution. We continued autonomy for a year . . . But to return to the CAP, there were platforms for demands: abolition of solitary confinement, abolition of court, abolition of isolation wards, visiting rooms, a decent salary for workers (equal to the minimum wage), proper medical and dental care—in short, platforms of ten points, but colossal as opposed to what we ask for now! We demand an extra shower, which is a bit of a shame . . . People who are incarcerated made their demands, the administration pushed back, or worse, didn't hear them out, they took action and totally torched the jails. In 1974, thirty-five jails were burnt, there were a hundred wounded and eight dead among the prisoners—today, no one remembers! It was an era where you could dream, believe that it was possible because it was the same in prison as in the street. There were thirty of us in CAP, but, for example, eight hundred at Colmar to support Serge Livrozet, who shouted, "Rotten French Justice!" Do you know of a call for anti-prison struggle where they number more than thirty today? Or else, we get help, because other people are there for something else, and just like that, we believe that we are eight hundred people.

I don't know much about Livrozet, I've only read **From Prison to Revolt***.*

Nicole: It's the best, a great book. You can also read *Scream (Hurle)* and *The Democratic Dictatorship* (*La Dictature démocratique*).
Jacques: In 1974, Livrozet was one of the main organizers of CAP, he debated everywhere, had sensational articles in the *Journal of Prisoners* that came out every month . . .
Nicole: Which was sold in the open in front of prisons and had a circulation of 5,000 to 10,000 copies.

Interview with Jacques and Nicole Lesage de La Haye

It was sold outside prisons?!

Jacques: Yes, but we were being picked up, thrown into the countryside, without transportation, getting home at three in the morning. The sales were very organized: there was a group from Fresnes, a group at the Santé, the group from Fleury … In 1974, there was also the mobilization at the Mende prison, against the isolation ward—at that time we called Mende "the capital of Lozère, and of torture." My 120 Vincennes students split into groups of thirty and sold all of the CAP journals throughout the University of Paris-VIII. It was so different from students and profs today, complicit with big business! Thanks to that, we were able to charter a bus filled with sixty militants, with the others traveling by car, and five hundred people circled the prison for an hour, with Livrozet talking to the prisoners with his megaphone—and they were responding. This action lived up to the struggles of the era. Each one was a blow. People inside truly fought, and those outside were effective. There was not this kind of comet tail of groups that can't get along with each other. There was a movement based in struggle, the anarchist movement of the Prisoner Action Committee (CAP), which led the head on fight against prisons.

Nicole: Today, there are lots of tiny factions, but it's pointless; there are too many disagreements. Before, when the CAP made a call, it was followed …

Nicole, were you also part of CAP?

Nicole: Yes, but towards the end. CAP lasted from December 1973 to February 1980. I joined in 1977. You have to understand that at the time, 10 to 15 percent of the prison population was fighting. But we weren't fighting for prisoners but rather against prisons, a totalitarian institution!

Jacques: We added the point that "all prisoners are political." In 1985, the Prisoner Labor Union (Association syndicale des prisonniers) consolidated common policies and rights when they claimed that every prisoner was primarily a social prisoner.

Nicole: This idea of social prisoners has been taken up today by the collective *Ne laissons pas faire* (Don't let them do it).

I would love if you speak a bit about your book, **La Guillotine du sexe** *(The Punishment of Sex).*

Jacques: You should know that, being a member of the convicts who were psychologically, emotionally, and affectively demolished by prison . . .

Nicole: Which incarcerated people don't want to admit!

Jacques: I was deeply ruined by my eleven and half years in prison. Among the causes of my breakdown, one of the prevailing factors was emotional and sexual frustration. Having done my studies in prison—high school, bachelors of arts in psychology—I chose as the subject of my doctoral thesis the emotional and sexual frustration of the incarcerated person. I never defended it; I worked, fought, and experienced so much that instead . . .

Nicole: And fucked . . . that you didn't have the time . . .

Jacques: Yes, but in order to make up for my eleven and half years of frustration, I'd have to fuck for fifty years! Even so, that didn't fix anything, there is a permanent lack, and in that respect, we come back to the Lacanian concept: you know you've finished therapy when you realize that you will always have a lack. That idea led me to interview sixty fellow incarcerated people, at the Central Prison of Caen: fifty inside and ten outside, on partial release. This resulted in the publication of the first edition of *La Guillotine du sexe* in 1978. It has been reissued twice, with the publisher Monde liberatire and then with the publisher Atelier. It attempts to explain why emotional and sexual frustration can end up creating a kind of cybernetic autoerotic circuit where the transmitter is their own receiver operating in a vacuum, which makes it so that after, they are unable to function in dual relationship. For them, the gaze of the other is an accusation. Their world is a world of solitude and despair. I called this overloading disorder, and I referenced some fifteen cases. The book did very well. I wanted to turn it into a novel, with a character similar to Bernard Tapie, his name is Gerald and he brilliantly gets out of jail after twelve years. But he's a complete mess with women, he just fucks up, because he is completely at odds emotionally and sexually with what he is socially. The work was not a success. There were only seven hundred copies of *L'Homme de metal* (*Metal Man*) sold, while *La Guillotine du sexe* sold eleven thousand copies. This was a very painful failure for me, because I thought that in the form of a novel it would be read more widely than as an essay.

Can you explain what the abolition of prison means to you practically?

Jacques: As anarchists, it is a principle: we can't accept any detention whether psychiatric, intellectual, carceral, the confinement of disability, etc.

Has there ever been a society without prisons?

Jacques: There are tribal societies. You read about that in *Tristes tropiques* by Claude Levi-Strauss.
Nicole: The Kanaks don't have prisons. Prisons exist become we created a consumer society where there is property . . .

Do you know of an anarchist experiment without prisons?

Nicole: No! Durruti opened the prisons, he gave the people inside a try. But he told them if they started up again, they had the right to a bullet in the head, it was a bit hasty!

Let's go back to the anti-prison argument.

Nicole: The only thing we must say is that if there were less social inequality, there wouldn't be prison, and if there was sexual education, there would be fewer problems of sexual deviancy. But let's go through it point by point. Let's talk about the sixty-one thousand incarcerated people. Firstly, prison is made for the poor. With more economic equality, you get rid of one part of the incarcerated people. Secondly, if you legalize drugs (like alcohol and medication today), a whole part of the prison population vanishes. Thirdly, 30 percent of the people are in prison for psychiatric reasons. They must be attended to. Finally, fourthly, in 1999, five thousand people were simply incarcerated for problems with their papers! They weren't criminals! If you add to that the people without papers who can't work and engage in criminal offenses . . . and then, realistically, there remain the true hooligans, predators, but who weren't always thugs, just delinquents.

Jacques: Charlie Bauer was a little delinquent in the northern neighborhoods of Marseille before becoming Mesrine's lieutenant . . .

Nicole: By reforming the national education a bit, there would only be 5 percent of incarcerated people remaining in prison. We would need to take measures to remove them, including psychological and educational support, so that they can return to public life without danger. But we would really have to look after them, take them into account! Whereas now, nobody cares about thousands of people in prison, they spend the day getting high on drugs, smoking dope, and watching television. Poor people come out even poorer than they were before, with diseases they caught in prison. Overnight, they find themselves on the street, with nothing! It's a vicious cycle. Society thinks it is protected this way—but it's a farce. If we did everything that we just mentioned, it would be a revolution. And that's what we are demanding! A different salary scale, a social revolution. And we can build all of this today, not in some future anarchist society!

Jacques: I'm going to add something that isn't at all opposed. Above all, we published a pamphlet on this idea, *Deviance in Anarchist Society (Déviance en société libertaire)*, Éditions ACL (1993). First, if we claim to be humane, what do we make of an institution where there is seven times the amount of suicide than in society as a whole? And in solitary, people commit suicide seven times more than in regular prison, thus forty-nine times more than outside! An institution like this can't be defended! Second, recidivism fluctuates between 50 and 70 percent. Is there a single business in capitalist society—because unfortunately we are in a capitalist society—that can withstand such failure? Third, regarding young people, it's more important. After first being inside, they have a recidivism rate of 50 percent. But once they go back in, the recidivism rate goes up to 70 percent. The people who go back in for three or more offenses have a recidivism rate of 90 percent. What do we make of an institution that fails at a rate of 90 percent? It is politically and economically unsustainable.

Now, let's bring back all of Nicole's arguments. People without papers, drug users, people in for economic crimes, lowering the wage rate from one to two instead of the current rate that goes from zero to one hundred. Everyone would have what they need to live. Those who want to work more would have a bit more. Painting, music, poetry—in short, creativity—would be considered a real job! In a society like ours, it is possible for everyone to make, from birth to death, between 1,200 to 2,000 euros. If we return to Nicole's calculation, the prison populations would go down to five thousand people inside!

And yet, I already hear the question, "what would you do if someone raped your daughter, you smartass abolitionist?" Well, the issue is settled theoretically. At the French Federation for Mental Health, they formed an ethics committee with Dr. Roland Broca and eighty French, Québécois, and Belgian specialists, on the treatment of sex offenders. I've done therapy with sex offenders. It's not what you hear in the media. The media is garbage; it's just about selling papers and getting better ratings. Reread *The Dictatorship of Ratings* (*La Dictature de l'audimat*) by Noël Mamère, he was saying the truth about it back then.

If you take care of those people, you are already beginning with the victim. You don't make demagogic political speeches ("vote for me, I will keep you safe, there will be no more victims"), human beings won't change, there will always be criminal tendencies because people want to possess, to take, to impose their law and their power. If we listen to the victims, what do they want? That you suffer and go to prison? Well, there is work to do in terms of prevention and education, but the suffering of the criminal is not going to repair the suffering of the victim. We must achieve true reparation—this is the idea with "*Ras les murs*," and it already began with the book *Lost Causes (Peines perdues)* by Louk Hulsman, published in 1982 by Centurion, and with the book by Maryse Vaillant, a psychologist and researcher with CNRS, *Reparation (La Réparation)*, published in 1999 by Gallimard. This is the person who allowed the Criminal Mediation Association to be set up in France, where the delinquent and victim really meet with each other. They ask the victim what they wish in terms of reparation, and it is often money, care, work for their house, their family, recognition of the suffering caused; but it's not incarceration, it's not slow death! An amazing thing! What do we find? That the people who have been criminals, including those with perverse characteristics, to say nothing about the greatest perverts that have no awareness of it, those who are called "disturbed psychopaths"— when they hear the victim's suffering, they return to what they have denied in themselves, their own suffering, what they experienced when they were little, which are at the root of their sex offenses. They are so destroyed that there is a period of decompensation, and at this time, we can encourage the encounter that will lead to a two-pronged therapy (with two therapists): medical and psychological treatment. The delinquent, shaken by the realization of the suffering caused to the other person, which plainly brings them to their own suffering, is ready for reparation. I treated a sex offender, his symbolic reparation involved working for a humanitarian organization. It is a long treatment, with follow-up, but it's effective. We must establish places for therapy, there is no point in imposing fifteen or twenty year prison sentences, because at the end of twenty-three years the person we release will rape and kill again. These kinds of sentences, they're simply complacency. Instead, when you notice they are doing better—and it's not the therapist who decides, but an external expert—they continue therapy outside. These guys are back in the streets and they don't assault anyone! Regarding this type of prisoner, those that they always try to shove down our throats, we just respond: two-pronged therapy in alternative locations.

We wanted to set up an alternative location in Val-de-Marne, we took the necessary steps, but it was refused for obvious political reasons. It would piss them off if the ultimate argument for the abolition of prison worked, because they need prison to exist in order to control the population and manipulate poor people. I will refer you to Loïc Wacquant's book *Prisons of Poverty* (*Les Prisons de la misère*). The best way to end poverty in capitalist society is to stuff them in prison ... Prison is a specter, a threat, one of the most powerful means of manipulation in a democratic dictatorship!

Can you talk a bit now about autonomy?

Jacques: In 1974, all the movements we just spoke about got together to create the Federation of Fringe Actions, (FLAM—Fédération de lutte des actions marginals). The leaders were so fucked in the head that it failed. Instead, a bit later in Vincennes, we created Marge (Fringe) in a more radical direction. It was all the anarchists, delinquents, drug users, non-citizens, people finishing psychiatric treatment, women, fags! Right away, we started a journal and mounted spectacular actions: occupying the Spanish, West German, and USSR embassies. We condemned the Franco regime, the authoritarianism of the RFA, especially the execution of the militants of the Red Army Faction (RAF). Our third occupation was of the Russian embassy to condemn the gulag. Walter Jones and I both ended up in jail. Our support committee was giant and the struggle was amazing. We got an appeal. During the hearing, between 150 and 200 people fought the Gardes Mobiles (National Guard) with crash barriers, and the two of us ended up with probation. After that, the department at Vincennes and the Ville-Évrard hospital wanted to fire me because of my criminal record. After a long struggle, we cleared my record. During this fight, we decided alongside the Libertarian Communist Organization (OCL) to establish an autonomous group to support the Red Army Faction lawyer who was incarcerated. The *Marge* journal spoke for the anarchist tendency called the "Wishers." Within the autonomous movement, there were three currents: the OCL, who were politicians; the "Comrades," made up of Marxist-Leninists, we called them the "miliatros" (tankies), and us, the "Wishers"—they called us the "Whackos." *Marge* was Stirnerian, but it also made reference to Bakunin, Voline, Kropotkin ... If anyone ever talked about the gulag in France, it was thanks to our action.

You were basically situs!

Jacques: We were absolutely Situationists. We did some totally crazy things. I'm thinking about a demo in 1981 where banners up front said "Put the Unemployed in Prison" and "No More Demos," as well as "Bring Back Slavery and Sexual Harassment [*le droit de cuissage*]."[1] We had some appalling pamphlets and slogans: "Rapists and Police Join Us." We danced and sang to "We Want to Die At Work." Now, that was a situationist demo, and we did plenty of others like it. In *Marge* and with the autonomous movement, we organized actions around psychiatry, sex work, prison, like the International Rally in Strasbourg in 1978, where we first tried out *Les Voltigeurs* [skirmish unit]: cowboys on motorcycles, armed with batons ...

Nicole: In Strasbourg, we saw for the first time how the cops could close down a city so as to prevent people from all over Europe from coming to protest. The German, Belgian, Swiss, and Italian autonomists were held at the borders, the bus of Parisian autonomists were stopped at a tollbooth. Eight hundred of us ended up corralled in a neighborhood facing off with twenty-five hundred riot cops. We had to run. The best example of our theoretical ideas was Europe's rejection of the cops.

And the Marge *journal?*

Jacques: We published issues on drug addiction, delinquency, women ...

Nicole: It wasn't just a journal, it was a group of people who lived together in a squat. We reappropriated from food stores ...

114

Interview with Jacques and Nicole Lesage de La Haye

Can we come back to the 1979 demo?

Nicole: The guys from Longwy were giants, and they were ravenous, filled with hate, they'd had enough. They left from Pantin in the morning...

You said that you were non-violent, but the common image of the autonomists is a guy with a helmet taking aim [le mec casqué qui va au carton]...

Nicole: When you are facing the State's tanks, even if you are non-violent, you can't just stand there holding a flower...

Jacques: We were hoping for a revolution, to redo 1968 but better! You can be generally non-violent, but when war breaks out, when there is insurrection, if you choose to be non-violent, you are complicit with the State that is going to crush your comrades. We wanted to overthrow the State, it was social war... To achieve a system of self-management that would be non-violent you have to stand against the cops, the tanks, the rulers... The day after the demo, I realized it had been doomed to failure. We dissolved the autonomist movement, *Marge*, and the CAP in 1980. We had people among us who were authoritarian, in love with power, we knew we'd end up fighting them. We only had the OCL between the Marxists and us. If we had taken power, we would have ended up murdering each other, killing ourselves down to the last one.

Nicole: Towards the end, you had as many autonomists as cops. And mind, it was super-macho—at the meetings, you only had guys talking.

Direct Action came from that, right?

Jacques: Direct Action came from the Comrades movement. When we dissolved everything, they said, "We're not stopping." They wanted to continue the struggle on the model of the Red Brigades (see *Direct Action: the First Years* [*Action directe, les premières années*] by Aurélien Dubuisson, Libertalia 2018).

The Abolition of Prison

We were just talking about your spiritual grandchildren in the 1980s, Bérurier Noir.2 Can we talk for a minute about the antipsychiatry struggle?

Jacques: You're thinking about the song, "Lobotomy." I did time, so did my brother. I watched him go crazy. He thought he was the Antichrist. He did twenty years, because he didn't receive any sentence reductions. I acted like a psycho in order to defend my brother and others who went mad in prison, it was a real massacre. The sector I worked in as a psychologist left the hospital, closed down. With the Asylum Information Group (Groupe information asile)—I was one of the founders in 1975 with Philippe Bernardet—we kicked up a real storm at the Ville-Évrard hospital about simple demands: take off the straitjackets, open the doors, stop the treatments that are just waiting for death. That leads to the deconstruction of the asylum. We started up a whole bunch of wacky activities: we invited musicians and started bands with the patients. Crazy stuff: forty-five harpists, the drummer from Taxi Girl, hard rock, punk, pop bands, all on the grounds of Ville-Évrard. One patient, Farid with blue eyes, told me, "This singer is crazy, Jacques. I'm not crazy, but him!" It was amazing, three hundred people, nurses, patients, musicians. We made a whole mess for thirty-one years, up to my retirement last September.

Nicole: The administration was at war with Jacques. They accused him of encouraging sexual relationships, they said that patients didn't like music, etc.

Jacques: We can treat people in alternative places of life. That is why we fought against imprisonment.

Notes

Chapter One: Why Prisons?

1. Michel Foucault, *Discipline and Punish: The Birth of the Prison*, trans. Alan Sheridan (New York: Vintage, 2012), 73.

2. Cesare Beccaria, *On Crime and Punishment*, trans. David Young (Indianapolis: Hackett, 1986), 51.

3. Dominique Vernier, *Peines perdues. Faut-il supprimer les prisons?* (Paris: Fayard, 2002), 7.

4. Ibid., 49.

5. Peter Kropotkin, *Words of a Rebel*, trans. George Woodcock (Montréal: Black Rose Books, 1992), 117.

6. Phillippe Paraire, "Introduction," in Peter Kropotkin, *In Russian and French Prisons*, trans. Pariare (Paris: Le Temps des cerises, 2009), 15.

7. Peter Kropotkin, *In Russian and French Prisons* (London: Ward and Downey, 1887), Chapter 10, https://theanarchistlibrary.org/library/petr-kropotkin-in-russian-and-french-prisons.

8. Angela Davis, *Are Prisons Obsolete*? (New York: Seven Stories Press, 2003), 16.

9. Ibid., 63.

10. Foucault, *Discipline,* 264 (translation modified).

11. Ibid., 265.

12. Fyodor Dostoevsky, *Memories of the House of the Dead*, trans. Jessie Coulson (Oxford: Oxford University Press, 2001), 16 (translation modified).

13. Victor Hugo, *The Last Day of a Condemned Man,* trans. Arabella Ward (Mineola, NY: Dover, 2009), 31 (translation modified).

14. Systems like halfway houses and electronic surveillance, *le régime de semi-liberté.*
15. L'Envolée, *Peines éliminatoires et isolement carceral, Pour en finir avec toutes les prisons* (Paris: L'Envolée, 2009), 3.
16. Ibid., 13.
17. Maurice Papon, convicted of crimes against humanity for aiding the deportation of Jews during Vichy.
18. L'Envolée, *Peines éliminatoires*, 40.
19. Ibid., 44.
20. Ibid., 88.
21. Ibid., 87.
22. Comité d'action des prisonniers. *QHS*, supplement to *Le CAPP* no. 56 (June 1978): 4.
23. Victor Serge, *Men in Prison*, trans. Richard Greeman (Oakland: PM Press, 2014), 20.
24. Ibid., 193.

Chapter Two: The Revolt of the Abolitionists

1. Catherine Baker, "Manifeste Abolitionniste" (March 1984), https://abolition.prisons.free.fr/manifeste.html.
2. Catherine Baker, *L'Abolition de la prison signifie-t-elle l'abolition de la justice, du droit et de toute société?* (Paris: Éditions du Ravin bleu, 1992), 15.
3. Ibid., 15.
4. France's second largest, more progressive magistrate's union, with ties to the Socialist Party.
5. The name could be understood as flight (carrying letters outside), or an upsurge.
6. The French title is *Peines éliminatoires et isolement carceral. Peines éliminatoire* etymologically refers to older punishments like exile, but has come to refer to imprisonment (removal) without the added ideology of penance, improvement, and so on that often excuse incarceration. Specifically it describes an imprisonment without possibility of parole—removal from society.
7. Samuel Gautier et al, "Abolir les prisons, ses mécanismes et ses logiques," *Mediapart* (June 4, 2014): https://blogs.mediapart.fr/edition/les-invites-de-mediapart/article/040614/abolir-la-prison-ses-mecanismes-et-ses-logiques
8. Ibid.
9. Ibid.
10. Kropotkin, *In Russian and French Prisons*, 370 (translation modified).
11. Ibid., 371.
12. Dennie Briggs, *In Place of Prisons* (London:Maurice Temple Smith Ltd, 1975), 63.

Notes

13. Ibid., 148.
14. The title is *Peines perdues*, which also could be translated as hopeless sentences or punishments.
15. Louk Hulsman and Jacqueline Bernat de Celis, *Peines perdues, le système penal en question* (Paris: Le Centurion, 1982), 150.
16. Catherine Baker, *Pourquoi faudrait-il punir?* (Paris: Tahin Party, 2004), 153.
17. Ibid., 155.
18. Ibid., 176.
19. Groupe Ras les murs, *Déviance en société libertaire, Prison et anarchie* (Paris: Atelier de creation libertaire, 1993), 44.
20. Albert Jacquard, *Un monde sans prison* (Paris: Le Seuil, 1993), 118.
21. Ibid., 205.
22. Ibid., 211.
23. Ibid., 213.
24. Ibid., 211.
25. *Journal des prisonniers* no. 2 (January 1973): 1.
26. *Journal des prisonniers* no. 9 (September 1973): 8.
27. Ibid.
28. Collectif, *Au pied du mur* (Paris: L'Insomniaque, 2000), 5.
29. Ibid., 295.
30. Ibid., 297.
31. Ibid., 300.
32. Ibid., 304.
33. Ibid., 316.
34. Ibid., 318.
35. Alain Brossat, *Pour en finir avec la prison* (Paris: La Fabrique, 2001), 78.
36. Ibid., 97.
37. Ibid., 103.
38. Gabi Mouesca, *Prison@net. Journal d'un "longue peine,"* (Paris: Gatuzain, 2002), 21.
39. Gabi Mouesca in Augustin Rosenstiehl and Pierre Sartoux, *Construire l'abolition.* (Paris: École d'architecture de Paris, "Carnets de Malaquais," 2005), 85.
40. Ibid., 147.
41. Ibid., 155.
42. Ibid., 175.
43. Ibid., 203.
44. L'Envolée, *Peines éliminatoires,* 93.
45. Davis, *Are Prisons Obsolete?,* 103.
46. Ibid., 112.

47. Jacques Colombat, *Du droit à l'évasion* (Paris: Riveneuve, 2014), 98.
48. Ibid., 98.
49. Hélène Erlingsen-Creste, *L'Abîme carceral, Une femme au sein des commissions disciplinaires* (Paris: Max Milo, 2014), 205.

Chapter Three: What Prison is Like

1. Éric Sniady, *Entre quatre murs, comment j'ai survécu trente ans dans l'enfer des prisons* (Paris: City, 2016), 173.
2. Ibid., 200.
3. Catherine, *Pourquoi faudrait-il punir?*, 48.
4. Collective, *Au pied du mur*, 199.
5. Ibid., 148.
6. Davis, *Are Prisons Obsolete?*, 48.
7. Sniady, *Entre Quatre Murs,* 136.
8. Ibid., 195.
9. Ibid., 223.
10. Ibid., 235.
11. Dominique Fauchet, "QI de Fresnes: c'est gràve docteur?," *L'Envolée* no. 4 (January 2002): http://journalenvolee.free.fr/envolee4/numero4/435.shtml.
12. Sniady, *Entre quatre murs,* 123.
13. Marcel Diennet, *Le Petit Paradis* (Paris: J'ai lu, 1972), 46.
14. Robin Cook in Abdel-Hafed Benotman, *Les Forcenés* (Paris: Rivages, 2000).
15. Daniel Gonin, *La Santé incarcérée* (Paris: L'Archipel, 1991), 88.
16. Ibid., 88.
17. Ibid.
18. Diennet, *Le Petit paradis.*
19. Ibid., 118.
20. Ibid., 120.
21. Ibid., 134.
22. Ibid., 133.
23. Ibid., 134.

Chapter Four: Sex and Prison

1. Jean Favard, *Dedans Dehors* (May 1998).
2. Arnaud Gaillard, *Sexualité et prison. Désert affect et désirs sous contrainte* (Paris: Max Milo, 2009), 293.
3. Nina Califano, *Sexualité incarcérée. Rapport à soi et rapport à l'autre dans l'enfermement* (Paris: L'Harmattan, 2015), 33.

Notes

Chapter Five: No Integration, No Re-entry

1. Jacquard, *Un Monde Sans Prisons*, 133.
2. Ibid., 133.
3. Ibid., 198.
4. Catherine Baker, *Pourqoui faudrait-il punir?*, 163.
5. Dennie Briggs, *In Place of Prison*, 147–8.
6. Dominique Vernier, *Peines Perdues*, 198.
7. Ibid., 283.
8. *Prisons, une humiliation pour la République*, June 29, 2000: http://www.senat.fr/rap/l99-449/l99-449.html.
9. Ibid., 237.
10. Loïc Wacquant, *Prisons of Poverty* (Minneapolis: University of Minnesota Press, 2009), 124.
11. Bruno Aubusson de Cavarlay "Hommes, peines et infractions: La Légalité de l'inégalité," *L'Année Sociologique* Troisième Série no. 35 (1985): 275–309.
12. Gabriel Mouesca, "Dossier prison: Gabriel Mouesca (OIP): 'L'abolition ne tient pas de l'utopie,'" interview with Union Communiste Libertaire, June 10, 2007, https://www.unioncommunistelibertaire.org/?Dossier-prison-Gabriel-Mouesca-OIP-L-abolition-ne-tient-pas-de-l-utopie.
13. Jean-Marie Domeanch, in *Esprit* no. 7–8 (July/August 1972): 47.
14. Kropotkin, *Words of a Rebel*, 163.
15. Sniady, *Entre quatre murs*, 234.
16. Léger (1937–2008) was convicted of killing a child in 1964 and served forty-one years—one of the longest terms served in Europe.
17. Califano, *Sexualité incarcérée*, 169.
18. Ibid., 189.
19. Ibid., 189.
20. Ibid., 312.
21. Gaillard, *Sexualité et prison*, 316.

Chapter Six: Alternatives to Incarceration: The Forerunners

1. Jacquard, *Un Monde sans prisons*, 211.
2. Briggs, *In Place of Prisons*, 108.
3. Ibid.
4. Ibid., 59.
5. Ibid., 124.
6. Ibid., 10.

Chapter Seven: Recent and Current Alternatives to Incarceration

1. Joan Hocquenghem, *Le Rendez-vous de Vicam* (Paris: Rue des Cascades, 2008), 137.
2. Yoloth Fuentes Sanchez, *Le Système de sécurité, de justice, de rééducation Communautaire de l'État du Guerrero comme système de justice parallèle de l'État du Guerrero* (PhD dissertation, *Faculté latino-américaine des sciences sociales,* Mexico), 16.
3. Ibid., 33.
4. Ibid., 50.

Chapter Eight: Mediation and Reparation

1. Davis, *Are Prisons Obsolete?* 113.
2. Natacha Filippi, *Brûler les prisons de l'apartheid* (Paris: Syllepse, 2012) 235.
3. Groupe Ras les murs, *Déviance en société libertaire,* 36.
4. Louk Hulsman, *Peines perdues,* 150.
5. Kropotkin, *In Russian and French Prisons,* Chapter 2 (translation modified).
6. In *Esprit, Toujours les prisons* no. 35 (November 1979): 112.
7. Albert Jacquart, *Un Monde sans prisons,* 187.
8. Ibid., 187.
9. Baker, *Pourquoi?,* 154.
10. Sanchez, *Le Système de sécurité,*33.
11. Ibid., 50.
12. Stéphane Jacquot, *La Justice réparatrice* (Paris: L'Harmattan, 2012), 18.
13. Jacquot, *La Justice réparatrice,* 22.
14. Robert Cario and Denis Salas, *Oeuvres de justice et victims,* volume I (Paris: L'Harmattan, 2001), 22.
15. Robert Cario and Denis Salas, *Oeuvres de justice et victims,* volume II: *Victimes: du traumatisme à la restoration* (Paris: L'Harmattan, 2001), 283.
16. Ibid., 297.
17. Robert Cario, *Les Rencontres détenus-victimes, l'humanité retrouvée* (Paris: L'Harmattan, 2012), 19.
18. Ibid., 122.
19. Ibid., 129.
20. Ibid., 156.
21. Jacquot, *La Justice réparatrice,* 59.
22. Maryse Vaillant, *La Réparation. De la délinquance à la découverte de la responsabilité* (Paris: Gallimard, 1999), 19.
23. Ibid., 86.
24. Ibid., 81.
25. Ibid., 24.

26. Cario and Denis, *Oeuvres,* volume II, 300.

Chapter Nine: How Do We Get Abolition?

1. Kropotkin, *In Russian and French Prisons*, Chapter 10.
2. Davis, *Are Prisons Obsolete?* 108.
3. Ibid., 107.
4. Ibid., 111.
5. Jacquard, *Un Monde sans prisons*, 205.
6. Ibid., 188.
7. Briggs, *In Place of Prison*, 144.
8. Ibid., 122.
9. Ibid., 53.
10. Ibid., 58.
11. Vernier, *Peines perdues*, 281.
12. Ibid., 243.
13. Ibid., 249.
14. Ibid., 250.
15. Ibid., 260.
16. Ibid., 249.
17. Fuentes Sanchez, *Le Système de sécurité,* 48.
18. Gaillard, *Sexualité et prison*, 322.
19. Ibid., 322.
20. Jean-Marie Domenach, *Esprit* no. 7/8 (July–August 1972): 54.
21. Cario and Salas, *Oeuvre de justice et victims,* vol. 1, 234.
22. Ibid., 236.
23. Colombat, *Du droit à l'évasion*, 101.
24. Ibid., 100.
25. Ibid., 94.
26. Ibid., 100.
27. Ibid.
28. James Guillaume, *Ideas on Social Organization*, https://www.revoltlib.com/anarchism/ideas-on-social-organization/view.php.
29. Guillaume, *Ideas*. [SB: I can't find the corresponding English, so translation is mine.]

Chapter Ten: Why Abolition?

1. Kropotkin, *Words of a Rebel*, Chapter 14. [SB: *sic* for antiquated pronouns.]
2. Vernier, *Peines perdues*, 283.

3.   Davis, *Are Prisons Obsolete?*, 75.
4.   Ibid., 113.
5.   Ibid., 129.
6.   Kropotkin, *In Russian and French Prisons*, Chapter 9 (translation modified).
7.   Davis, *Are Prisons Obsolete?*, 78.
8.   Ibid., 99.
9.   Vernier, *Peines perdues*, 270.
10. Rosenstiehl and Sartoux, *Construire*, 203.
11. Kropotkin, *In Russian and French Prisons*. Chapter 2 (translation modified).
12. Jacquard, *Un monde sans prisons*, 193.
13. Kropotkin, *In Russian and French Prisons*, Chapter 2 (translation modified).
14. Ibid., Chapter 9 (translation modified).
15. Baker, *Pourquoi.*, 172.
16. Hulsman, *Peines perdues,* 124.
17. Ibid., 124.
18. Ibid., 68.
19. Jacquard. *Un monde sans prisons*, 68.
20. Baker, *Pourquoi faudrait-il punir?*, 179.
21. Davis, *Are Prisons Obsolete?*, 16.
22. Ibid., 43.
23. Briggs, *In Place of Prison*, 10.
24. Jean-Marie Domenach, *Esprit* no. 7/8 (July–August 1972).
25. Peters in Cario and Salas, *Oeuvre de justice et victims,* volume 1, 240.
26. Davis, *Are Prisons Obsolete?*, 106.
27. Brossat, *Pour en finir*, 118.
28. Comité d'action des prisonniers, *QHS*, 55.
29. Mouesca in Rosenstiehl and Sartoux, *Construire,* 6.
30. Collectif, *Au pied du mur*, 295.
31. Ibid.
32. Ibid.

Interview with Jacques and Nicole Lesage de La Haye

1.   *Le droit de cuissage* is used today to refer to sexual harassment or abuse of power, but it refers to the idea of *droit du seigneur* or *jus primea noctis*, a supposed medieval right for the feudal lord to have sex with women in their fief, particularly on their wedding night.
2.   French 80s anarchist punk band. Bérurier is a character from Frédéric Dard's novels, Noir refers to the black of anarchy. Their shows were often followed by riots.

Bibliography

Aubusson de Cavarlay, Bruno. "Hommes, peines et infractions: La Légalité de l'inégalité," *L'Année Sociologique* Troisième Série, no. 35 (1985): 275–309.

Baker, Catherine. *L'Abolition de la prison signifie-t-elle l'abolition de la justice, du droit et de toute société?*. Paris: Éditions du Ravin bleu, 1992.

———. "Manifeste Abolitionniste," March 1984, https://abolition.prisons .free.fr/manifeste.html.

———. *Pourquoi faudrait-il punir? Sur l'abolition du système pénal*. Paris: Tahin Party, 2004.

Bazin, Hervé. *La Fin des asiles*. Paris: Grasset, 1959.

Beccaria, Cesare. *On Crime and Punishment*. Translated by David Young. Indianapolis, In.: Hackett, 1986.

Botton, Pierre. *Prison*. Paris: Michel Lafon, 1997.

Briggs, Dennie. *In Place of Prison*. London:Maurice Temple Smith Ltd, 1975.

Brossat, Alain. *Pour en finir avec la prison*. Paris: La Fabrique, 2001.

Califano, Nina. *Sexualité incarcérée. Rapport à soi et rapport à l'autre dans l'enfermement*. Paris: L'Harmattan, 2015.

Cario, Robert. *Les Rencontres détenus-victimes, l'humanité retrouvée*. Paris: L'Harmattan, 2012.

Cario, Robert and Denis Salas. *Oeuvres de justice et victims*, volume I. Paris: L'Harmattan, 2001.

———. *Oeuvres de justice et victims,* volume II: *Victimes: du traumatisme à la restoration.* Paris: L'Harmattan, 2001.

Collectif. *Au pied du mur, 765 Raisons d'en finir avec toutes les prisons.* Paris: L'Insomniaque, 2000.

Colombat. Jacques. *Du droit à l'évasion.* Paris: Riveneuve, 2014.

Comité d'action des prisonniers. *QHS,* supplement to *Le CAPP* no. 56 (June 1978): 4.

Cook, Robin. In Abdel-Hafed Benotman, *Les Forcenés.* Paris: Rivages, 2000.

Davis, Angela. *Are Prisons Obsolete?.* New York: Seven Stories Press, 2003.

Diennet, Marcel. *Le Petit Paradis.* Paris: J'ai lu, 1972.

Dostoevsky, Fyodor. *Memories of the House of the Dead.* Translated by Jessie Coulson.Oxford: Oxford University Press, 2001.

L'Envolée. *Peines éliminatoires et isolement carceral, Pour en finir avec toutes les prisons.* Paris: L'Envolée, 2009.

Erlingsen-Creste, Hélène. *L'Abîme carceral, Une femme au sein des commissions disciplinaires.* Paris: Max Milo, 2014.

Esprit no. 7-8. July/August 1972.

Esprit, Toujours les prisons, no. 35. November 1979.

Fauchet, Dominique. "QI de Fresnes: c'est gràve docteur?," *L'Envolée* no. 4 (January 2002). http://journalenvolee.free.fr/envolee4/numero4/435.shtml.

Favard, Jean. *Dedans Dehors.* May 1998.

Filippi, Natacha. *Brûler les prisons de l'apartheid.* Paris: Syllepse, 2012.

Foucault, Michel. *Discipline and Punish: The Birth of the Prison.* Translated by Alan Sheridan. New York: Vintage, 2012.

Fuentes Sanchez, Yoloth. *Le Système de sécurité, de justice, de rééducation Communautaire de l'État du Guerrero comme système de justice parallèle de l'État du Guerrero* (PhD dissertation, *Faculté latino-américaine des sciences sociales,* Mexico).

Gaillard, Arnaud. *Sexualité et prison. Désert affect et désirs sous contrainte.* Paris: Max Milo, 2009.

Bibliography

Gautier, Samuel et al. "Abolir les prisons, ses mécanismes et ses logiques," *Mediapart,* June 4, 2014. https://blogs.mediapart.fr/edition/les-invites-de-mediapart/article/040614/abolir-la-prison-ses-mecanismes-et-ses-logiques.

Goffman, Erving. *Asylums: Essays on the Social Situation of Mental Patients and Other Inmates.* Oxford: Taylor & Francis, 2017.

Gonin, Daniel. *La Santé incarcérée. Médecine et conditions de vie en detention.* Paris: L'Archipel, 1991.

Groupe Ras les murs. *Déviance en société libertaire, Prison et anarchie.* Paris: Atelier de création libertaire, 1993.

Guillaume, James. *Ideas on Social Organization,* https://www.revoltlib.com/anarchism/ideas-on-social-organization/view.php.

Hocquenghem, Joani. *Le Rendez-vous de Vicam.* Paris: Rue des Cascades, 2008.

Hugo, Victor. *The Last Day of a Condemned Man,* trans. Arabella Ward. Mineola, NY: Dover, 2009.

Hulsman, Louk and Jacqueline Bernat de Celis. *Peines perdues, le système penal en question.* Paris: Le Centurion, 1982.

Jacquard, Albert. *Un monde sans prison.* Paris: Le Seuil, 1993.

Jacquot, Stéphane. *La Justice réparatrice, quand victims et coupables échangent pour limiter la récidive.* Paris: L'Harmattan, 2012.

Journal des prisonniers, no. 2. January, 1973.

———. no. 9, September 1973.

Kropotkin, Peter. *In Russian and French Prisons.* London: Ward and Downey, 1887.

———. *Words of a Rebel.* Translated by George Woodcock. Montréal: Black Rose Books, 1992.

Lesage de La Haye, Jacques. "Un État sans prison," *Esprit, Toujours les prisons,* no. 35. November 1979.

———. *La Machine à fabriquer les délinquants.* Paris: Éditions Lesage de La Haye, 1982.

———. *L'Homme de metal.* Paris: Eistences, 1995.

———. *La Guillotine du sexe. La vie sexuelle et affective des prisonniers.* Paris: L'Atelier, 1998.

Livrozet, Serge. *De la prison à la révolte.* Paris: Mercure de France, 1973.

Monneareau, Alain. *La Castration pénitentiaire. Droit à la sexualité pour les prisonniers.* Paris: Lumière et Justice, 1986.

Mouesca, Gabriel. Dossier prison: Gabriel Mouesca (OIP): "L'abolition ne tient pas de l'utopie" (June 10, 2007). https://www.unioncommuniste libertaire.org/?Dossier-prison-Gabriel-Mouesca-OIP-L-abolition-ne -tient-pas-de-l-utopie.

———. *Prison@net. Journal d'un "longue peine,"* Paris: Gatuzain, 2002.

Mucchielli, Laurent, *Violences et insécurité. Fantasmes et réalités dans le débat français.* Paris: La Découverte, 2002.

Paraire, Phillippe. "Introduction," in Peter Kropotkin, *Dans les prisons russes et françaises.* Translated by Paraire. Paris: Le Temps des cerises, 2009.

Rosenstiehl, Augustin and Pierre Sartoux. *Construire l'abolition.* Paris: École d'architecture de Paris, "Carnets de Malaquais," 2005.

Sénat. *Prisons, une humiliation pour la République.* June 29, 2000. http://www.senat.fr/rap/l99-449/l99-449.html.

Serge, Victor. *Men in Prison.* Translated by Richard Greeman. Oakland: PM Press, 2014, epub.

Sniady, Éric. *Entre quatre murs, comment j'ai survécu trente ans dans l'enfer des prisons.* Paris: City, 2016

Vaillant, Maryse. *La Réparation. De la délinquance à la découverte de la responsabilité.* Paris: Gallimard, 1999.

Van Daal, Julius. *Beau comme une prison qui brûle, une émotion Populaire en 1780.* Paris: L'Esprit frappeur, 1998.

Vernier, Dominique. *Peines perdues. Faut-il supprimer les prisons?.* Paris: Fayard, 2002.

Wacquant, Loïc. *Prisons of Poverty.* Minneapolis: University of Minnesota Press, 2009.